NYMPH FLY-TYING TECHNIQUES

Jim Schollmeyer

Nymph *Fly-Tying* Techniques

Jim Schollmeyer

Frank **Amato**

PORTLAND

ACKNOWLEDGEMENTS

This book was made possible by the many fly tiers who shared their
knowledge, and Tony Amato with his great layout skill, thank you.
Ted Leeson edited, set me straight when necessary, and served me
beer and chips whenever I needed moral support.
Ted, I can't thank you enough.

Published in 2001 by Frank Amato Publications, Inc.
P.O. Box 82112, Portland, Oregon 97282
(503) 653-8108 • www.amatobooks.com

Softbound ISBN: 1-57188-266-9   Softbound UPC: 0-81127-00102-6
Spiral Hardbound ISBN: 1-57188-267-7   Spiral Hardbound UPC: 0-66066-00456-7

All photographs taken by the author unless otherwise noted.
Book Design & Layout: Tony Amato

Printed in Singapore

3 5 7 9 10 8 6 4 2

TABLE OF CONTENTS

Chapter 2:
Lashed and Extended Bodies 56

Chapter 3:
Strand Bodies 62

INTRODUCTION

When I was first asked to write a book on tying nymphs, I was reluctant. There were already a number of very good pattern books, and I wasn't really sure that another one was justified. But when I began thinking about nymph patterns, and tiers I have watched, and my own tying, one thing stood out—the way many patterns have evolved from variations on a handful of basic designs and tying techniques. And it occurred to me that something useful might be written demonstrating how such evolutions take place and how a tier's repertoire of flies can be broadened, not by learning dozens of new patterns, but by seeing how a variety of modifications can be worked into fly designs to produce the desired appearance or behavior.

The result is this book, and while it contains a number of patterns that I have found effective in my own fishing, it is really less a pattern book than a fly design book. Its purpose is,

first, to illustrate the many different body styles used to tie nymphs, and second, to show how new patterns can be created from that original style by adding, or subtracting, or altering a variety of fly components. The techniques pictured here can certainly help you tie most of the standard nymph patterns, but its real aim is to help you tie flies that fit your own tying and fishing style. Most tiers do this to some extent already, substituting materials, improvising, combining existing designs, trying new things just to see how they look or work. This tinkering around is what makes fly tying fascinating and is how great patterns come to be. This book is an attempt to systematize that process a bit, to illustrate the great variety of possibilities that can be used in this tinkering.

Since this book takes a slightly different approach to tying flies, a few words on how the presentation is set up will simplify its use.

Chapter 1 presents the tying techniques used to dress the nymph patterns shown in this book (and, in fact, many other types of fly patterns as well). Since many of these techniques are used to tie a number of the flies shown, it seemed most efficient to illustrate them once in this chapter, and then refer the reader back to these basic instructions whenever they are needed, making Chapter 1 a kind of reservoir of tying methods.

Since the body of the fly is the basic skeleton on which a pattern is fleshed out, Chapters 2 through 6 are organized around the different body styles used to produce different types of nymphs. The heading on the left-hand page describes the body style and the material used to dress it. Two fly photographs are also shown on the left-hand page. The fly shown on the green background is the main pattern, the basic style that can be modified. The fly shown on the blue background is an alternate version of the fly, a kind of first evolution. The steps for tying each of

these patterns are shown on backgrounds of the corresponding color. The dressing for each is below its photograph and often includes optional materials or components, for subsequent modifications to the pattern. These variations are pictured on red backgrounds and are followed by the instructions for dressing them. Some tying steps include instructions in boldfaced type, followed by a page number that refers you back to Chapter 1, where the technique needed at that point is presented in more detail.

This book does not illustrate the flavor-of-the-month nymph patterns, or even my own favorites. It is intended as a guide to help you tie the patterns included here and also patterns that you find in other books, or to copy flies purchased in a shop or given to you by friends. But most of all, I have designed the book in a way that I hope will encourage and help you to create your own nymph designs, and to translate ideas into effective fishing flies.

Chapter 1

Basic Tying Techniques

The methods shown in this chapter are used in tying the flies in the following chapters. A fly tier using these methods will be able to tie most nymph patterns. Learning these methods will also give you a good foundation for learning other tying methods and techniques.

HOOKS

Hooks come in all sizes and shapes; they are the bases on which the flies are built. The choices are often overwhelming for the novice fly tier. Most manufacturers have catalogues that give a description of the hooks they carry, and the containers hooks are sold in almost always have a description of the hook on the cover. Once a few basic terms are learned, it is easy to choose the right hook for the fly to be tied.

Most of the hooks shown in this book are tied on barbless hooks. This was done for a reason. Catch and release has become very common in most waters, and pinching down the barb on a hook may weaken it or even break it; so most manufacturers are making many of the most popular barbed hooks available in barbless form as well.

Hook Descriptions

The hook wire diameter is defined starting with the Standard (S) as the basic hook. The same hook one size lighter and finer is 1 extra fine, 1 XF or 1 X fine, two sizes finer is 2 extra fine, 2XF, 2X fine. Thus, a #14 1XF hook has a wire diameter equal to a #16 standard hook; a #14 2XF hook is equal in wire diameter to a #18 standard hook. The same hook that is one size heavier and stronger is 1 extra heavy, 1XH, or 1X heavy, two sizes heavy is 2 extra heavy, 2XH, or 2X heavy.

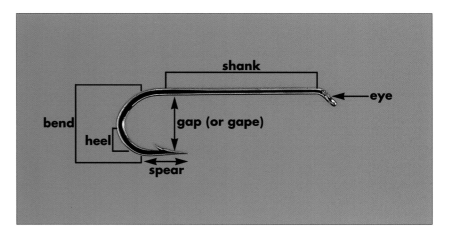

Nymph Hook Lengths
1 XL, 2 XL, 3 XL

The length of the hook shank is also defined by a standard length (S) for the basic hook. The same hook one size shorter is 1 extra short, 1XS, or 1X short and so forth. The same hook that is one size longer is 1 extra long, 1XL, or 1X long, two sizes longer is 2 extra long, 2XL, or 2X long and so forth.

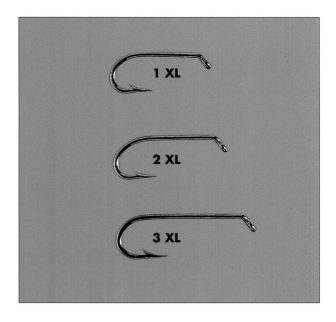

Nymph, Scud, Pupa, and Swimming Nymph Hooks

Hook shapes vary, and for this book I use the hook descriptions that are often on the hook containers—nymph, scud or pupa, and swimming nymph. The shape of the hook gives the finished fly it shape, so choose the hook shape to match the fly you are tying.

Hook eyes vary in the direction they come off of the hook shank. Most nymph hooks are down eyed, but again the choice is yours; try to match the hook eye to the fly you are tying. Inspect the eye of each hook to make sure there is no gap where it is pinched against the hook shank. A gap in a hook eye that is not fully closed may cause the leader knot to break; discard such hooks or close the gap with pliers.

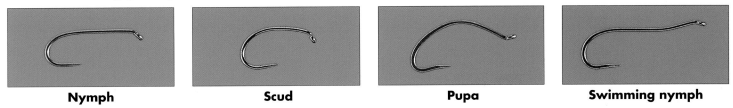

Nymph **Scud** **Pupa** **Swimming nymph**

DE-BARBING HOOKS

It is best to remove the barb from a hook before you tie the fly; if you break the point after tying the pattern, the fly is worthless. Following are three ways to remove the barbs; pliers are used in two methods and a file in the third. You should test each brand of hook with the following methods to see which one produces the best result without damaging the hook point. If the hook barb breaks during de-barbing, use the filing method to remove the rest of the barb.

Parallel De-barbing Pinch

Of the two pinch methods, this method, when done properly will produce the flattest barb with the least amount of stress to the hook. With this method, you can also hold the hook with your fingers while de-barbing it.

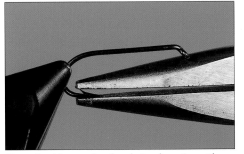

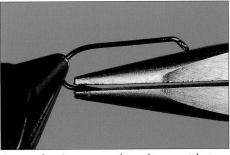

Step 1: Mount the hook in the vise. Place the lower jaw of flat needle-nose pliers against the bottom of the hook spear with the end of the plier jaws a little beyond the barb. Do not pinch the bend of the hook; it may break.

Step 2: Squeeze the pliers with just enough pressure to pinch the barb down. It is normal to have a small bump where the barb was; do not try to flatten it or you may break the hook.

Perpendicular De-barbing Pinch

With this method, care must be used during the pinch or you will break the hook or not completely flatten the barb.

Step 1: Mount the hook in the vise. Position the needle-nose pliers crosswise over the hook spear. The lower jaw of the pliers should support the whole length of the spear without touching the bend of the hook.

Step 2: Use light pressure to pinch the barb down.

Filing Barbs

This method requires a small, thin, sharp, fine-toothed file to work properly. This de-barbing method causes the least amount of stress to the hook point and it completely removes the barb. This method works best with larger hooks. But it is not as quick as the other methods and so it is probably the least used.

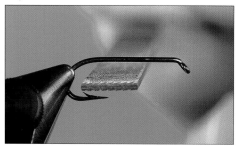

Mount the hook in the vise, clamping it on the upper part of the bend, to increase the working area. You do not want the file cutting into the vise jaws.

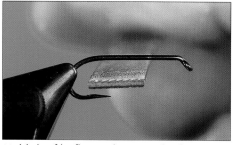

Hold the file flat and perpendicular to the hook shank and gently stroke it across the barb to remove it. Take care not to catch the hook point with the file, which will damage the point, or to file into the hook bend, which will weaken the hook.

SHARPENING HOOKS

Most fly fishermen carry hook sharpeners while fishing to repair a hook damaged while fishing. But it is a good idea to check the sharpness of your hooks before tying a fly on them; bare hooks are the easiest to sharpen. Hooks smaller than #10 are usually sharp enough right from the box; larger hooks should be checked for sharpness. If one hook in a package is dull, chances are the rest of them will be too. A small, fine-toothed file or one of the specialty hook sharpeners can be used to sharpen the hook.

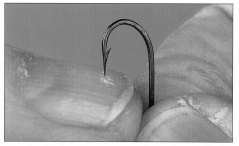

To check the sharpness of the hook, hold the hook as shown and lightly press the point against your thumbnail; then gently pull it across the nail. A sharp point will stick and resist moving. A dull point will slide across the nail.

To sharpen the hook, mount it in the vise as shown. Hold the file to match the taper of the point; gently stroke the file across the surface. This stroke will keep a burr from forming on the point. File both sides and the bottom of the spear.

Mounting the Hook

Many hooks have a tapered spear, which provides a poor clamping surface for mounting the hook in the vise. Mounting the hook by its "heel" where the wire diameter is uniform produces a good gripping surface and maximizes the working area around the hook. Test the grip on the hook by pushing down on the hook eye. If the hook slips, tighten the tension of the jaws.

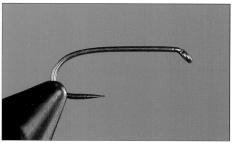

Place the hook in the vise and loosely grip it by the "heel" so that the tips of the vise jaws extend a little beyond the hook wire. Align the hook shank so it is parallel with the working surface, and then tighten the jaws.

THREAD HANDLING

THREADS

Most modern manufactured threads used for fly tying are either nylon or polyester. They are available either waxed or unwaxed. Waxed thread frays less than the unwaxed, but the unwaxed is a little easier to spin flat, so the choice is yours. Try both so you become familiar with their characteristics. For tying trout flies, the most common thread sizes are A, 3/0, 6/0, 8/0, 12/0, 14/0. Size A thread is the thickest and strongest; from there the threads drop in diameter and strength to size 14/0, which is the finest thread with the lightest breaking strength. Choose the thread size to match the hook size and materials used. The thread should be thin enough to reduce bulk but strong enough to hold the materials. Use thread sizes A and 3/0 on large hooks or for spinning hair. Thread size 6/0 matches well with hook sizes 4-12. Size 8/0 should be used with hook sizes 14-18.

TIE IN

This method is also known as the "single-wrap thread mount method". It is a simple and easy way to mount the thread to the hook shank. To illustrate the method, wire is used in place of tying thread.

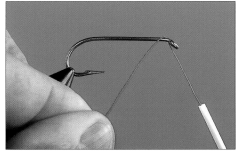

Step 1. Mount the hook in the vise. Pull 6 inches of thread from the bobbin and fold it over hook shank as shown.

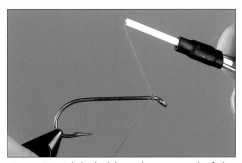

Step 2. While holding the tag end of the thread, wrap the bobbin thread around the hook shank, angling the wrap to the rear. This will trap the hand-held thread against the hook shank. Take two thread wraps around the hook shank.

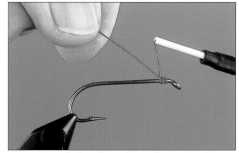

Step 3. Lift the thread as shown and continue winding the thread with 3-5 tight wraps toward the rear. The thread wraps will slide down the thread ramp producing close tight wraps.

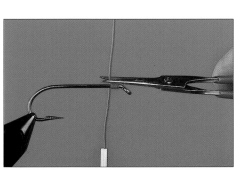

Step 4. To trim the thread, lift the thread perpendicular to the hook shank and cut the thread close to the hook shank.

Controlling Thread Twist

When thread is wrapped in the normal direction around a hook shank, it acquires one clockwise twist for each wrap. If the thread is twisted too tightly it will break. This is normally not a problem for a fly tier, because as you pause to prepare or arrange materials for the next tying operation, the hanging bobbin slowly unwinds and removes the added twists. But it is important to understand the properties of twisted and untwisted or flat thread, since these are useful in tying.

By spinning a hanging bobbin in a clockwise direction, the thread fibers tighten into a tight cord. Tightly twisted thread has a smaller, more uniform diameter, resists fraying, and is stronger than its untwisted, flattened form. When wrapped, tightly twisted thread quickly builds up bulk, which is desirable for forming small underbodies or heads. When wrapped over the hook shank, it forms a rough, non-slip base for tying in materials. One problem with tightly twisted thread is that if the tension is remove from the twisted thread, it will furl or twist back on itself; this property makes it difficult to mount materials using the soft-wrap method (p. 17).

Thread that is twisted in the counterclockwise direction will flatten when wrapped. This property is useful in a number of ways. When mounting a material using the soft wrap method and tension is removed from the flattened thread, it is easy to control the placement of the thread. Also, flattened thread wraps are smoother and produce less bulk than twisted thread wraps. The drawbacks of flattened thread are that the strands tend to wander, they are prone to catching or breaking, and the wraps form a slippery base for mounting materials.

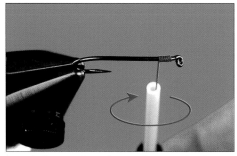

To tighten the thread, spin the hanging bobbin by its barrel in a clockwise direction.

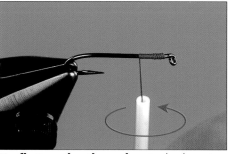

To flatten the thread, spin the hanging bobbin by its barrel in the counterclockwise direction. Watch where the thread contacts the hook shank and you can tell when the thread is completely flat. Don't spin the bobbin further or the thread will twist in the opposite direction.

TIE OFF

Following are a number of methods used to secure the thread to the hook shank after completing the fly or to lock in mounted materials before going on to the next step. Use 2-3 half-hitches to secure material that is located back from the hook eye. Half-hitches can also be used to complete head of the fly; place the knots close together to form a smooth head. The whip-finish is used to tie off the thread behind the hook eye to complete the fly; this strong knot forms a smooth neat head.

Half-hitch

This method, also known as the "two-finger half-hitch", allows the tier good control over where the knot is placed.

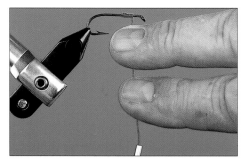

Step 1. With the bobbin hanging at the desired knot position, grip the bobbin with your left hand. Place the first two fingers of your right hand against the thread as shown.

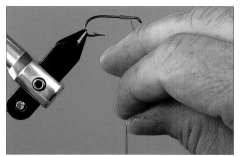

Step 2. Pinch the thread with your right thumb and forefinger as shown.

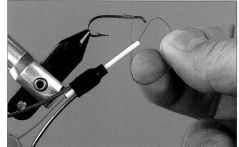

Step 3. While keeping tension on the hanging thread with your middle finger, rotate your right hand so the palm is facing you. This will form a loop as shown.

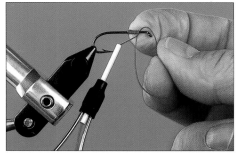

Step 4. While pinching the loop to keep tension on the thread, place the top of the loop over the hook eye and position it next to the hanging thread. Then with your right forefinger pinch the loop against the far side of the hook shank.

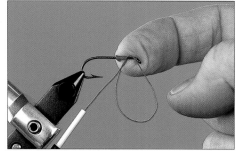

Step 5. Remove your middle finger from the loop.

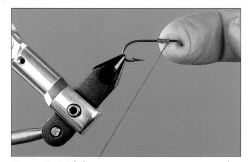

Step 6. While maintaining pressure on the loop against the hook shank, slowly pull down on the bobbin to tighten the knot.

Hand Whip-finish

This finishing method requires no whip-finishing tool, but it does take a little practice to learn.

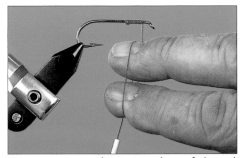

Step 1. Strip about 6 inches of thread from the bobbin. With the back of your hand facing you, wrap the thread, forming a loop, around the first two fingers of your right hand.

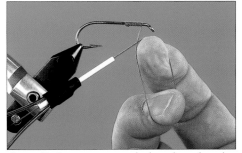

Step 2. Rotate your right hand so that the palm points upward; angle the bobbin to the rear. Now the mounted thread should be perpendicular to the hook shank and the bobbin thread should be in front of the mounted thread.

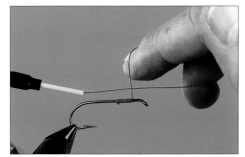

Step 3. Move your fingers above the hook, rotate your palm downward and raise the bobbin above the hook shank. The bobbin thread is now horizontal and crosses the vertical mounted thread.

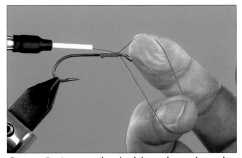

Step 4. Lower the bobbin thread to the hook shank. While twisting your wrist until your palm faces you, use the index finger to guide the vertical bobbin thread around the hook shank.

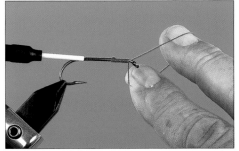

Step 5. While maintaining tension on the loop with your fingers, rotate your wrist so the back of your hand is facing you. Don't wrap the thread; let your fingers slide inside the stationary loop.

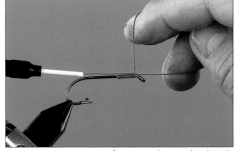

Step 6. Raise your fingers above the hook shank with your palm facing down. One thread wrap is now binding down the horizontal thread. Your hands are now in the same position as shown in Step 3.

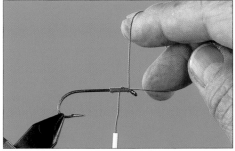

Step 7. Repeat Steps 4-6 four more times to place four more wraps around the horizontal thread. After the last thread wrap, let the bobbin hang.

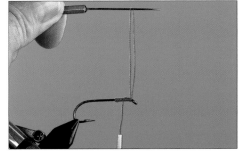

Step 8. With your left hand, place a dubbing needle into the loop. Transfer the tension of the loop to the needle as you remove your fingers from the loop.

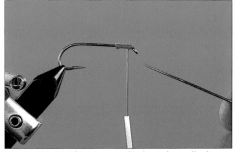

Step 9. With your right hand, pull down on the bobbin as you use the needle to guide the knot to the desired position. When the needle touches the hook shank, remove it; tighten the knot and cut the thread close to the hook shank.

Orbiting Tool Whip-finish

There are two types of whip-finisher tools; both are easier to learn than the hand whip-finish method. The Matarelli tool used here has a sleeved grip. The grip spins on its handle when tying a knot, causing the hooked arm to "orbit" around the hook shank as it wraps the thread.

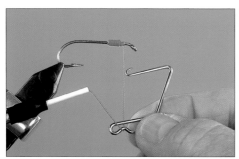

Step 1. Hold the whip-finisher above the handle to keep it from turning and position the tool, hook end up, beside the hanging thread. Lift the bobbin and catch the thread in the guide notch on the arm.

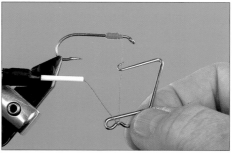

Step 2. Catch the thread with the hook, so its point is behind the hanging thread.

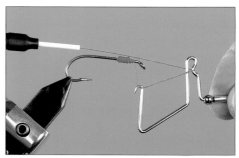

Step 3. Slide your fingers down onto the handle sleeve. Keep tension on the thread, raise the bobbin, and lay the thread on top of the hook shank. The handle will remain stationary, as the tool spins to the position shown.

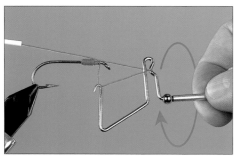

Step 4. While holding only the handle, use a cranking motion to move the tool clockwise one turn. Keep the guide notch in line with the hook shank, as the hooked end of the tool wraps the thread around the hook shank.

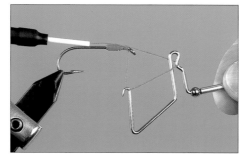

Step 5. Repeat Step 4 four more times. If more thread is needed, rock the tool back and forth to draw more thread from the bobbin.

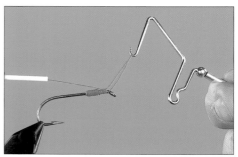

Step 6. After the last wrap, slip the thread from the guide notch. Pull on the bobbin to tighten the thread, while using the hook to guide the thread into position. Unhook the tool when it touches the knot and pull on the bobbin to seat the knot.

BROKEN THREAD

No one is immune from breaking the tying thread while tying a fly. If the tag end is long enough, immediately use it to take 2-3 half-hitches around the hook shank. Then tie in the bobbin thread and take 2 wraps over the tag end of the broken thread, and trim the excess.

When thread breaks because it has been nicked by the hook point, it is usually too short to knot. When this happens, grip the tag end of the broken thread with hackle pliers and use the following procedure to save the fly.

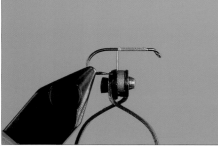

Step 1. Grip the broken thread with hackle pliers. If any loose wraps developed when the thread broke, either unwind them or apply light pressure on the thread and rock the thread back and forth to remove the slack.

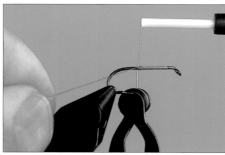

Step 2. Tie in the bobbin thread in front of the broken thread. Red is used to show the different threads.

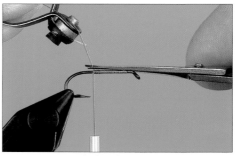

Step 3. Wind the thread back over the broken thread, locking it to the hook shank. Trim the tag ends close to the hook shank.

Finishing the Thread Wraps

Head cement sold in fly shops is usually a type of lacquer, varnish, or fingernail polish. These adhesives are used to cement tie-off knots to keep them from unraveling. Head cements are not strong adhesives, but when properly applied they are adequate. Viscosity, which determines how the head cement flows, is the most important property of head cement. Head cements are sold in thin or thick forms. Once a cement container is opened and used, the cement will thicken after a period of time and needs to be thinned. Use the proper thinner for the cement.

Thinned cements are easy to apply, soak into the thread wraps, and dry fast. One coat of thinned cement that penetrates the thread is normally all that is needed to hold the knotted thread in place. If a smooth head is desired, then additional coats can be used; make sure, though, each coat has dried before applying the next coat or you will end up with a poor bond and tacky head.

Thicker cements penetrate poorly and should not be used to secure the thread wrap; they can be used as the finishing coat on the thread wraps for a smoother head on larger flies.

MOUNTING MATERIALS

Following are a few basic mounting techniques that can be adapted to mount most materials.

Soft Wrap
This is the most commonly used mounting method and the easiest to learn.

Step 1. Position the material (Antron yarn is used here) over the mounting position. Spin the bobbin counterclockwise to flatten the thread (p. 14). Take one loose wrap over the material at the tie-in position. Do not tighten the wrap.

Step 2. After completing the first wrap, pull the bobbing directly toward you and apply more pressure to the thread. The material should now be held in place.

Step 3. Take 2-3 more close, tight wraps in front of the first. The material should now be locked in place.

Angle Wrap
This technique is well suited for mounting stiff or slippery materials.

Step 1. Hold the material (calf tail is used here) at a 45-degree angle over the tie-in position. Using moderate tension on the thread, take one wrap around the material and hook shank.

Step 2. While still maintaining moderate pressure on the thread, take another wrap directly in front of the first wrap and pull it tight. As the thread is tightened, move the material in line with the hook shank.

Step 3. Take 2-3 tight, close thread wraps in front of the previous wraps to lock the material in position.

Shank Wrap

This technique is used to bind the material to the top, bottom or sides of the hook shank. When done properly it forms a smooth underbody.

Step 1. Use either of the previous methods to mount the material on the hook shank at the tie-in position. Lift the material and take a tight wrap over the material.

Step 2. Pull down on the bobbin to tighten the thread, and at the same time pull the material slightly toward you. This will keep the material centered on top of the hook shank.

Step 3. Continue the thread wraps as shown in the Steps 1-2 until the tie-off position is reached.

Slide Mount

This variation of the soft-mount method is used to position a material on the hook shank after it is mounted but before it is firmly secured. To slide materials that are too short to grip with your fingers, use hackle pliers.

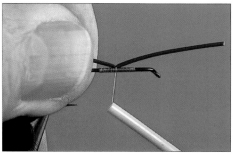

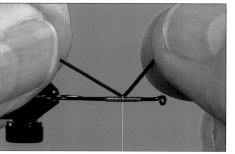

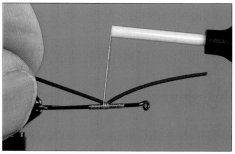

Step 1. Use the soft wrap method shown above to take two loose thread wraps over the middle of the material (rubber legs are shown here) at the tie-in position.

Step 2. With the bobbin hanging below the tie-in position, use your fingers to grip the material and slide it into position—in this case, on the side of the hook.

Step 3. Once the material is properly positioned, use your fingers to adjust the length. Then take 2-3 tight thread wraps over the previous wraps to lock the material in place.

Pinch Wrap

This wrap is used to mount materials on top of the hook shank. It is particularly useful in counteracting the tendency of some materials to roll off the top of the hook shank under thread pressure.

Step 1. Use your right fingers to position the desired length of material (squirrel hair is used here) directly over the hanging bobbin at the tie-in position.

Step 2. While your right fingers hold hair in place, use your left thumb and forefinger to pinch the hook shank and hair, together, directly over the tie-in position as shown.

Step 3. With your right hand, spin the thread counterclockwise to flatten it; this will help you control the thread. Lift the thread on the near side of the hook shank and slide it between your thumb and the hair.

18

Step 4. While maintaining the pinch, form a small loop on top of the hair. Without closing the loop, slip the thread between the hair and your forefinger on the far side of the hook shank.

Step 5. While maintaining the pinch, pull straight down on the thread to tighten the wrap, which will bind the material to the top of the hook shank.

Step 6. Repeat Steps 3-5 to place one more thread wrap over the material. Then move your fingers and check the position of the material. Small adjustments can be made at this point.

Step 7. If you're are satisfied with the position of the material, pinch it at the mounting position and repeat Steps 3-5 to place one or two more thread wraps over the material.

Step 8. Slide your left fingers back so they are positioned directly behind the thread wraps, and take 2-3 close, tight wraps in front of the other wraps.

TRIMMING MATERIALS

Sharp scissors are a must for the close trim cuts that are needed to make a neat looking fly. Scissors with a serrated blade are less likely to disturb the position of slippery materials when cutting.

Basic Trim

This method is used on materials with little bulk that can be trimmed close to the thread wraps without producing a noticeable step or edge.

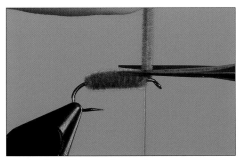

Top trim. For a close trim on top of the hook shank, lift the material straight up from the hook shank. Lay the scissors on top of the thread wraps and cut the material.

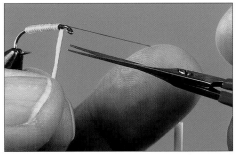

Bottom trim. Pull 2-3 inches of thread from the bobbin. Pull the material straight down and use your middle finger to move the thread off to the side, keep it clear of the scissors. Cut the material close to the thread wraps.

Angle Cut

Angle cuts are used to taper the edge that is formed when bulky materials are cut.

Step 1. Pinch the material and slide the scissors under the material as shown.

Step 2. Pull the material along the axis of the hook shank. Position the scissors at the desired angle to the material. Here a shallow angle is used to produce a long taper.

Step 3. While maintaining tension on the material, trim it to a taper.

UNDERBODIES

Underbodies are used to shape the body of the finished fly. Almost any material can be used to form an underbody. The most commonly used material is lead wire or lead-free wire, which is also used to weight the fly. When bulk without weight is needed, a yarn underbody is a good choice.

Direct-Wrap Lead Underbody

Any wire can be used with this technique. For the best results, use wire that is approximately the same diameter as the hook-shank wire. There are waters where lead, even lead wire, is prohibited, so use lead-free wire whenever possible. To reduce waste, a bobbin should be used to hold the wire. Use a pair of fine-tipped wire cutters to trim the wire.

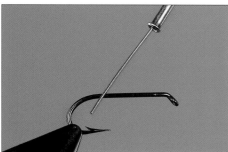

Step 1. Pull 2-3 inches of wire from the bobbin and position the tag end across the hook shank as shown.

Step 2. With your left fingers, pinch the wire against the hook shank and wrap the wire forward with close tight wraps.

Step 3. Cut the wire close to the hook shank. Tie in the thread at the front of the hook shank and form a smooth taper at the front of the wire wraps. Then wrap the thread over the wire and form a taper at the rear of the wire wraps.

Double-layer Lead Underbody

This technique uses two layers of wire to add weight and bulk to the underbody. By wrapping the second layer over the entire length of the shank or over the thorax only (as shown here), you can match the body profile of a number of naturals.

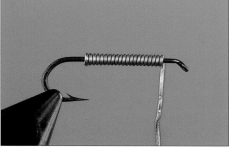

Step 1. Use the direct-wrap lead underbody method shown above to form the first layer. Stop 4-5 wraps behind the hook eye.

Step 2. Angle the wire to the rear and add the second layer. Stop the wraps at the end of the thorax area; continue the wraps to the rear if a uniform body shape is desired.

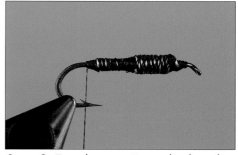

Step 3. Trim the wire. Tie in the thread at the front and form thread tapers at the front and rear of the wire wraps.

Flattened Wire Underbody

If a flatter body shape is desired, lead or lead-free wire underbodies can be flattened by squeezing them with smooth-jawed pliers. Do not over-flatten the body or you may break the thread.

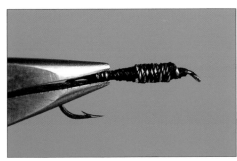

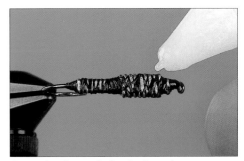

Step 1. Use one of the methods above to form the underbody, and then tie off and clip the thread. Starting at one end, gently squeeze the pliers to flatten the body to the desired shape, and continue over the rest of the body.

Step 2. Have the pliers' jaws pinch the wire at an angle; to produce a uniform body shape, reverse the hook and repeat Step 1.

Step 3. The underbody thread wraps may have been damaged during the flattening process; coat the underbody with CA glue to secure the body.

Strand Underbody

A lightweight underbody can be formed with any lightweight stranded material. Yarn, such as the Antron shown here, is ideal for forming large underbodies. Thread or floss works well for smaller flies. For a properly shaped underbody, the diameter of the underbody material, when tightly twisted, should be close to the size of the hook wire.

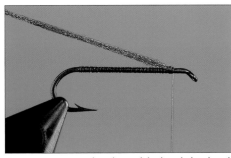

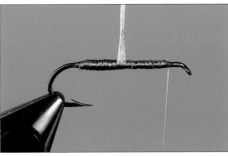

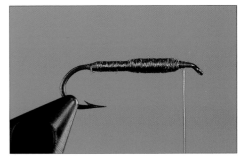

Step 1. Tie in the thread behind the hook eye and wind it over the length of the hook shank; then return the thread to the front of the hook shank. Mount the yarn at the tie-in position and trim the excess.

Step 2. Wrap the yarn in layers to form the body shape. The size of underbody should be about half the size of the finished fly.

Step 3. After forming the underbody, tie off the yarn and trim the excess.

PREPARING MATERIALS

Preparing Feathers

Feathers plucked from a bird skin should be cleaned of the fluffy barbs or fibers found on the lower part of the stem. Barbs used for tails or legs must be aligned and separated from the stem of the feather.

Step 1. Pull a feather from a neck or saddle (a hen feather is shown here). Hold the stem above the fluff with your left fingers, and use your right fingers to pinch the fluffy barbs close to the feather stem.

Step 2. Pull down on the barbs to strip them from the stem.

Step 3. Repeat Steps 1-2 until all of the fluffy barbs are removed from the feather. If the feather is intended to hackle a fly, it is now ready to be mounted. If the barbs are to be used for tails or legs, continue with the following steps.

Aligning and Cutting Barbs

Feather barbs that are to be used for tails or legs should be aligned for a neat looking fly. The following steps show how to align and remove a bundle of fibers from a feather.

Step 1. Use your left fingers to hold the prepared feather by the tip. With your right thumb and forefinger lightly pinch the barbs below your left fingers and stroke downward. Repeat until the barbs stand out perpendicular to the stem.

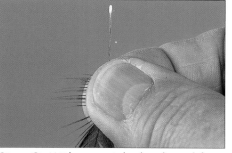

Step 2. With your right thumb and forefinger, pinch the desired quantity of barbs close to the feather stem.

Step 3. Pinch the aligned tips with your left thumb and forefinger. Cut the barbs close to stem. You can pull the barbs from the stem as shown in the previous method, but the barbs may shift out of alignment as you pull.

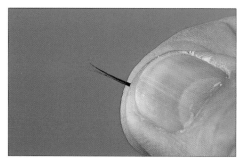

Step 4. Use your right thumb and forefinger to carefully gather the barb ends into a bundle. They are now ready for mounting.

Preparing Hair

Hair that is used for tails or legs needs to be removed from the hide, cleaned of its underfur, and aligned at the tips by using a hair stacker. Hair used for spun or stacked bodies just needs to be clipped from the hide and the underfur removed.

Step 1. Use your left fingers to gather a bundle of hair. Cut the hair close to the hide.

Step 2. Grip the hair bundle by the tip and pull out any loose hairs and underfur.

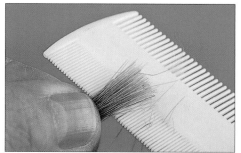

Step 3. With a small fine-toothed comb (a flea comb available at a pet shops is used here), remove the rest of the underfur. The hair is now ready for stacking or for forming a hair body.

Stacking and Aligning Hair

After the underfur has been removed from the cut hair, the tips need to be aligned; the easiest way to do this is with a hair stacker. Stackers come in different sizes; the mid-sized one shown here will work well for most nymph patterns. A hair stacker needs to be cleaned periodically with an anti-static laundry sheet to keep the hairs from clinging to the stacker.

Step 1. Cut and clean a bundle of hair as shown in the previous method. Insert the hair, tips first, into the barrel of the hair stacker.

Step 2. Hold the stacker as shown. Make sure your forefinger completely covers the opening. Tap the bottom of the stacker sharply against the table top 3-4 times to align the hair tips. Coarse or kinky hair will need more taps.

Step 3. To consolidate the bundle, tilt the stacker at a 45-degree angle and lightly tap it a few times against the tabletop.

Step 4. Use your left hand to move the stacker into a horizontal position. With your right hand carefully remove the barrel from the stacker, keeping it in the horizontal position.

Step 5. Grasp the exposed hair tips with your left fingers and remove the hair from the barrel.

Step 6. Transfer the aligned hair bundle to your right fingers for mounting.

TAILS

On nymph patterns, tails may be made from a large number of different materials. The following methods or variations of them should enable you to mount any type of material used to form nymph tails. The lengths of tails vary with the type of insect you are imitating. If you are unsure of the length, consult a picture of the natural (p. 52) and note the ratio of tail length to body length. Use this same proportion on the imitation.

Bundled-fiber Tail

For nymph tails, it is best to use solid-fiber materials with this method.

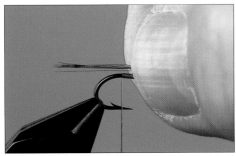

Step 1. Position the hanging thread 1-2 thread wraps from the start of the hook bend. **Align and cut** (p. 20) a bundle of feather barbs. Use your right fingers to hold the bundle with the desired tail length extending behind the tie-in position.

Step 2. With your left thumb and forefinger, pinch the bundle over the tie-in position. Use the **pinch wrap** method (p. 18) to mount the bundle of barbs with 3 tight thread wraps.

Step 3. Check the alignment of the tail; small adjustment can be made at this time.

Step 4. After checking the tail, pinch the bundle directly behind the thread wraps and take 2-3 wraps forward to lock the barbs in place.

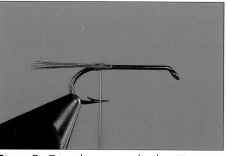

Step 5. Trim the excess barbs. You can leave the tag ends exposed and cover them later with the body material, or you can cover them with thread wraps at this time.

Dubbing Ball Split Tails

Both single or bundled fiber materials can be used with this method to produce a divided tail. Solid non-flaring materials, such as the Micro Fibetts used in the following demonstration, produce the best tails. For smaller flies, a thread ball can be used in place of the dubbing ball to split the tails.

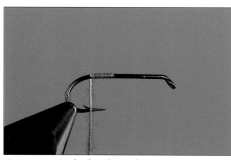

Step 1. With the thread at the tie-in position, spin a small amount of dubbing on the thread.

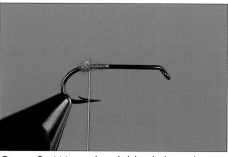

Step 2. Wrap the dubbed thread over the hook shank in layers to form a ball of dubbing at the tie-in position. For small flies, 1-3 wraps should be enough to form the ball; on larger flies more wraps may be needed.

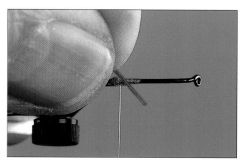

Step 3. Position the thread directly in front of the ball. Cut a small bundle of Micro Fibetts and grip them at the desired tail length. Place the bundle at a 45-degree angle over the tie-in position, as shown in this top view.

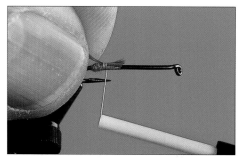

Step 4. Spin the thread counterclockwise (p. 13) to flatten the thread. Then use the **soft-wrap** method (p. 17) to mount the fibers to the side of the hook shank. Slight adjustments can be made to the fibers at this time.

Step 5. Prepare another bundle of fibers like the first. Position it over the hook shank so that it matches the length of the first bundle.

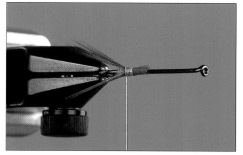

Step 6. Mount the bundle as shown above in Step 4. Then spin the thread clockwise to tighten it. Wrap the thread to the rear, stopping as it touches the dubbing ball; this will lock the tails in position. Trim the excess fibers.

Split Biot Tails

Goose biots are often used for tails on stonefly nymph patterns. When the biot is mounted with its concave side facing outward, it will flare outward on its own.

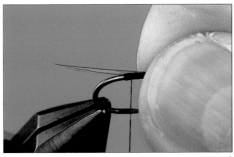

Step 1. Lay a thread base to the rear of the hook and wind the thread forward five wraps. Cut 2 matching biots from a strip. Use your right fingers to position a biot on the far side of the hook shank, with its concave side facing outward as shown.

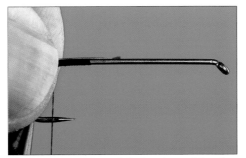

Step 2. With your left thumb and forefinger, pinch the biot to the side of the hook shank just behind hanging thread.

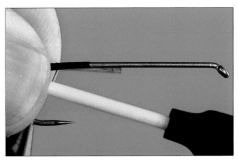

Step 3. Spin the bobbin counterclockwise to flatten the thread. Take 2 loose wraps over the hook shank and biot. Tighten the thread after the second thread wrap by pulling the bobbin straight toward you.

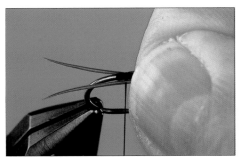

Step 4. Remove your fingers from the biot; at this time slight adjustments can be made to align the biot. With your right fingers, place the second biot on the near side of the hook shank, with its concave side facing out, and align it with the first.

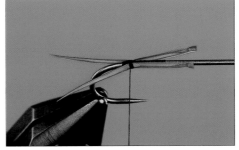

Step 5. Repeat Steps 2-3 shown above; slight adjustments can be made on the near side biot at this time.

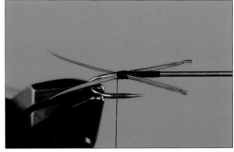

Step 6. Pinch the biots behind the rear thread wraps. Wrap the thread to the rear, stopping at the rearmost thread wrap.

Split Rubber Tails

Rubber tails are common on larger nymph patterns and are being used more often on smaller nymph patterns as finer rubber becomes more available.

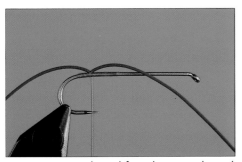

Step 1. Lay a thread foundation to the tail position, and wrap the thread forward 6-8 wraps. Cut a 2- to 3-inch length of rubber leg material and center it over the hanging thread. Secure it with 3 thread wraps.

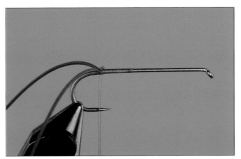

Step 2. Take the forward tag end and fold it back on the near side. Take 3 thread wraps over the fold.

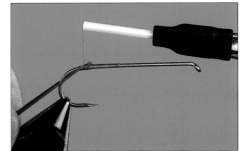

Step 3. Grasp both tags of rubber and pull them to the rear and downward, so that one tag is on each side of the hook shank. Take 3 thread wraps to the rear; this will secure the tags to the sides of the hook shank.

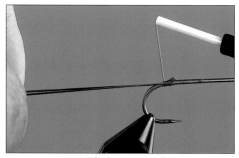

Step 4. Now lift the tag ends so they are in line with the hook shank and pull with equal tension on both ends to stretch them. Take 3-4 tight thread wraps toward the rear over the stretched rubber.

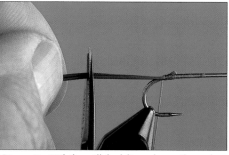

Step 5. While still holding the tails, relax the tension on them. Measure the length for the tails and cut both pieces of rubber at the same time, so they will be of equal length.

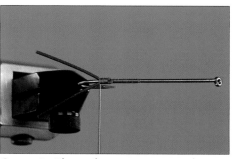

Step 6. The tails are now complete. It should be noted that stretching the rubber strands as they were secured in Step 4 causes the tail strands to flare outward.

BODIES

The following methods are used to form bodies for the fly patterns shown in this book.

DUBBING

Dubbing is a technique that involves placing natural or synthetic fibers on thread or wire and spinning them into a yarn that can be wrapped on the hook. The following dubbing methods, once learned, will allow you to use the dubbing of your choice to create a variety of body styles.

Preparing Dubbing Materials

Most tiers use packaged dubbing. But there may be times when you want to mix dubbing of different shades to produce a color more to your liking, or to cut some fur from a hide to use as dubbing, or to produce a dubbing from cut lengths of yarn. All of these fibers must be mixed to produce a dubbing of uniform color and texture.

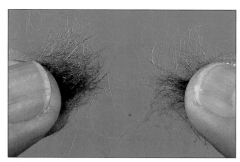

Finger Mixing. A small amount dubbing may be mixed this way. Pinch the material in one hand and use the other hand to pinch and pull some material from the clump. Stack one half atop the other, and repeat the process until the material is mixed.

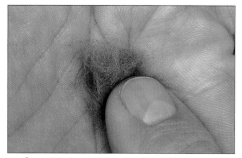

Palm Mixing. To mix short fibers or fur, place a small amount of material into your left palm. Use your right forefinger to gently mix the material. Do not press too hard with you finger or you will roll the material into a cord.

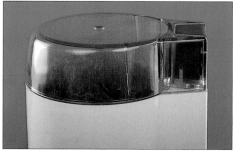

Coffee Grinder Mixing. To mix large quantities of dubbing, use an electric coffee grinder. Mix the dubbing with short pulses and do not overload the mixing chamber. Clean the mixing chamber with anti-static laundry sheet after each use.

Direct Dubbing

With this method, each pinch of dubbing is placed on the thread and spun separately. This technique is best suited for fine to medium-textured dubbing. Dubbing spun clockwise will tighten as the tying thread twists during wrapping; dubbing spun counterclockwise will loosen during wrapping, and may require periodic re-spinning to keep the dubbing from unraveling.

Step 1. Position the thread at the point you wish to begin dubbing. Hold the bobbin in your right hand with the dubbing pinched between the thumb and forefinger as shown.

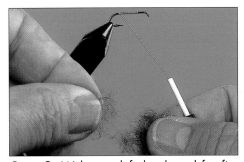

Step 2. With your left thumb and forefinger, "tease" a small amount of dubbing from dubbing held in your right fingers.

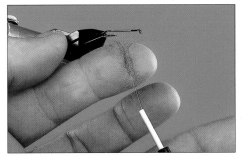

Step 3. Lift the bobbin, pull it toward you, and hold it with light tension. With your left fingers, place the teased dubbing against the back of the thread close to the hook shank. The thread should cross the pad of your forefinger.

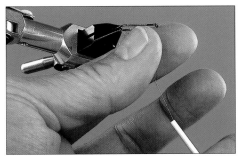

Step 4. Place your left thumb over the dubbing. Roll the dubbing and thread down your finger. Roll the dubbing in one direction only; reposition your fingers and repeat the roll until the dubbing is spun into a cord. This clockwise spin produces a tight cord.

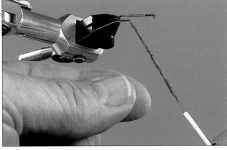

Step 5. Repeat Steps 2-4 until the desired length of thread is covered with dubbing. Try to produce an even cord, fill in any thin areas and remove dubbing from thick areas. A sparsely dubbed thread will produce a neater body.

Step 6. Dubbed thread should be wrapped in layers to form the body. A thin spot on dubbing cord may require a few wraps over the same area to fill it out. For thicker areas on the dubbing cord, space the wraps more widely to even out the dubbing.

Waxed Thread Direct Dubbing

A waxed thread is used to hold the dubbing material in place before it is spun into a cord. This method works well with any dubbing. The dubbing shown in following method is spun in a counterclockwise direction. This will produce a looser cord and a shaggier body, but the dubbing must be spun after every couple of wraps to keep the it from unraveling. If a tight cord and body wrap is desired, twist the dubbing clockwise on the thread.

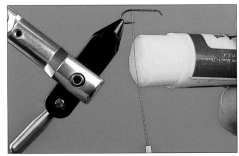

Step 1. With the thread at one end of the area to be dubbed, pull about 3 inches of thread from the bobbin. While keeping light pressure on the thread, apply a thin film of wax over the thread. Remove any large clumps of wax.

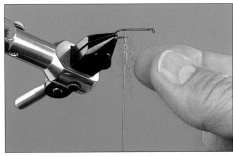

Step 2. Tease out a small pinch of dubbing and touch it against the backside of the waxed thread. Remove your fingers. The dubbing will adhere to the thread.

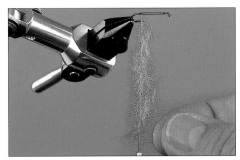

Step 3. Repeat Step 2 until the desired length of thread is covered. Make sure a uniform amount of dubbing is applied along the thread so that an even cord will be formed after spinning.

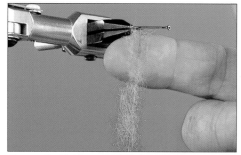

Step 4. With your left hand, lift the bobbin and pull it toward you and hold it under light tension. Place your right forefinger behind the dubbing, so the thread crosses the middle of the pad as shown.

Step 5. Place your thumb over the dubbing and roll it down your finger. Roll in one direction only. Reposition your fingers and repeat the roll until the cord is formed to your satisfaction.

Step 6. Move your fingers down the thread to the next area to be spun, and repeat Steps 4-5 until all of the dubbing is spun into a cord and ready to wrap.

Dubbing Loops

A dubbing loop, formed from a strand of thread or wire, is used to trap the dubbing so it can be spun into a yarn. Any type of dubbing can be used with dubbing loops. There are a number of commercial tools that are made to aid tiers in producing dubbing loops, but for the following methods a dubbing hook is all that is needed. To form a dubbing loop noodle see Muskrat (p. 112).

Direct Dubbing Loop

This is a variation of direct dubbing using a dubbing loop to tighten the cord. It is most useful with soft- to medium-textured dubbing. This method can be used to form distinctly segmented bodies.

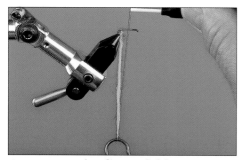

Step 1. Use the **direct dubbing** method (p. 27) to dub a length of thread. With a dubbing hook, catch the thread below the dubbing and return the thread to the hook shank in front of the hanging thread.

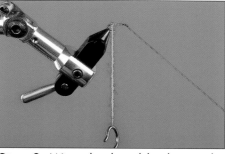

Step 2. Wrap the thread back over the hanging thread to form a loop; then advance the thread to the forward tie-off position. Using the dubbing hook, spin the loop clockwise to tighten the dubbing into a tight cord. Do not overtighten the loop or it will break.

Step 3. Wind the dubbed cord forward to the tie-off position.

Forming a Dubbing Loop

A dubbing hook is needed for the following methods.

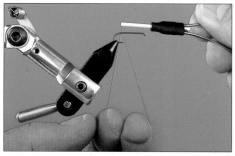

Step 1. Wrap the thread to the rear of the area to be dubbed. Pull 8-12 inches of thread from the bobbin and wrap it around the first two fingers of your left hand; then bring the bobbin thread back to the hook shank in front of the hanging thread.

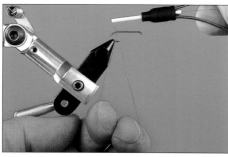

Step 2. While maintaining light tension on the looped thread, wrap the thread toward the hook bend until you have captured the base of the hanging thread with 1 or 2 wraps.

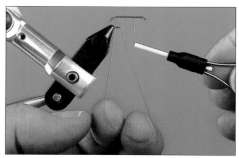

Step 3. Wrap the thread to the forward tie-off position. The loop is now ready for the dubbing to be added.

Trapped-Loop Dubbing

This is the most commonly used dubbing-loop technique. You can add any texture of dubbing to this loop.

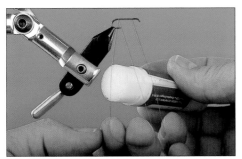

Step 1. Form the dubbing loop as shown in the previous method. Apply wax to one side of the loop.

Step 2. With your right fingers, apply dubbing evenly along the waxed thread.

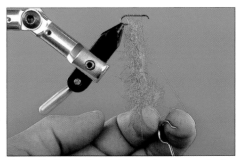

Step 3. With the dubbing hook, catch the bottom of the loop between the fingers, as shown.

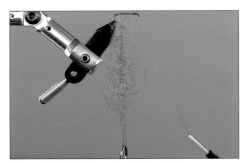

Step 4. While maintaining light pressure on the loop with the dubbing hook, carefully remove your fingers from the loop. The dubbing is now trapped between the threads of the closed loop.

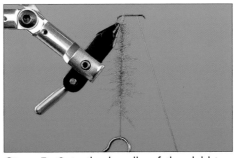

Step 5. Spin the handle of the dubbing hook clockwise until the desired tightness of the cord is reached.

Step 6. Wrap the body and secure the loop at the tie-off position. On larger flies it may be necessary to dub the body in sections, forming a new loop after the wrapping and tying off the previous one.

Dubbing Teaser

A dubbing teaser is a tool that is used to pick out the dubbing of a wrapped body to give it a shaggy appearance. There are a number of commercial dubbing teasers available, but it is simple to make one that will work for all but the smallest flies.

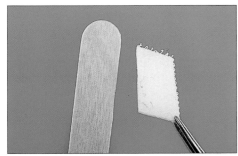

Step 1. You will need a Popsicle stick and the "hook" side of a square of self-adhesive Velcro.

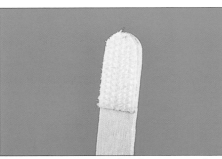

Step 2. Remove the backing paper from the Velcro. Place the Velcro on the stick and trim the excess. You now have a dubbing teaser that will rough up dubbed bodies without cutting the thread.

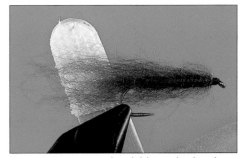

Step 3. Tease out the dubbing, by brushing it with the Velcro hooks until you produce the desired shagginess.

Wire-core Dubbing Brushes

Wire-core dubbing brushes are similar to trap-loop dubbing in that the material is trapped between two strands and spun. The difference is that wire-core dubbing brushes are formed before the fly is tied. There are a number of ways to produce these brushes. A few very good commercially made dubbing-brush tools are available to fly tiers, but for this book we are going to use a homemade board that will produce all of the dubbing brushes needed for the flies that appear here.

The material used and the density of its application will determine the shape of the dubbing brush. If dubbing fibers taken from a hide or cut from yarn are laid perpendicular to the wire, the finished brush looks like a strand of large chenille. This type of dubbing brush, often called "fur chenille," is probably the most widely used.

Use a medium- to fine-gauge wire to form the dubbing brushes.

Making a Flat Dubbing Board

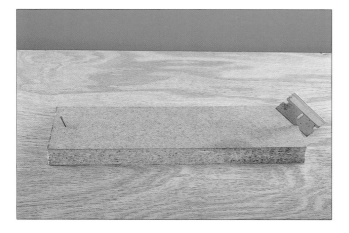

Cut a piece of 1/2-inch particleboard (its rough surface helps hold the dubbing in place) 6-8 inches long and 3-4 inches wide. At one end, in the center of the board, drive in a 1-inch finishing nail about halfway in at the angle shown and cut off the head. At the other end of the board, directly in line with the nail, cut a small slit in the edge of the board with a razor blade.

Dubbing Brush

Using the dubbing board with mixed dubbing that is placed uniformly over the wire will produce a dubbing brush that gives a dense, durable body. For more working room, place the board on a book.

Step 1. Take 3-5 wraps of wire around the nail and stretch the wire over the board. Lift the wire and apply a thin coat of wax over it.

Step 2. Place the stretched, waxed, wire on the board and slip it into the slit to secure it. Place the wire spool on the book, and hang a dubbing hook on the wire below the slit.

Step 3. Take a pinch of dubbing and place it on the board, centered over the waxed wire.

Step 4. Continue applying an even layer of dubbing to the rest of the waxed wire. While holding the dubbing hook, lift the spooled end of the wire and carefully lay it over the dubbing. With light tension on the wire, take 3-4 turns around the nail.

Step 5. With the dubbing hook under light tension, gently remove the wire from the slit. Spin the dubbing hook to start twisting the wire. As the dubbing starts to twist, lift the wire so the twisting fibers clear the board.

Step 6. With little tension on the wire (too much tension will break the wire), continue twisting the wire until the brush reaches the desired texture. Remove the wire from the nail; the brush is now ready to use.

Fur Chenille Dubbing Brush

Using pinches of fur cut from the hide and laying then perpendicularly across the wire with the tips aligned will produce a fur chenille after it is twisted. Pre-cut strips of squirrel or rabbit work well for this method. The texture of the chenille is determined by the position of the hair on the wire.

Step 1. Prepare the dubbing board as shown in Steps 1-2 of the previous method. Align the fur tips on a strip of hide and cut them next to the hide.

Step 2. Place the fur across the wire. Use your fingertip to gently drag the fur down the wire to evenly distribute it. The thickness of the fur layer will determine the density of the chenille.

Step 3. Continue placing the fur on the wire until the desire length is reached. Take time to adjust the fur so it is uniform in density and the tips are aligned.

Step 4. Use Steps 4-6 of the previous method to finish the brush. For spiky chenille, as shown here, position the butt ends of the hair close to the wire.

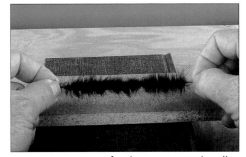

Step 5. For a soft, dense, even chenille, as shown here, position the fur so that the wire crosses the hair about 1/3 of the way up from the butt end.

Yarn Chenille Dubbing Brush

The dubbing board can be used to produce a yarn chenille that can be wrapped as a fly body, hackle, or gills. Most yarns can be used, but Antron yarn produces the best results with this technique. If the brush is to be used as hackle or gills, lay a thin layer of material on the wire to make a sparse chenille.

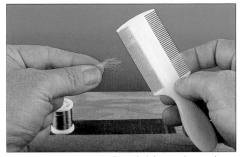

Step 1. Prepare the dubbing board as shown in Steps 1-2 of the **dubbing brush** method. Take a length of yarn and use a fine comb to separate the fibers.

Step 2. Cut about 1/2-inch material from the combed fibers and center them on the wire. Continue until the desired length of wire is covered.

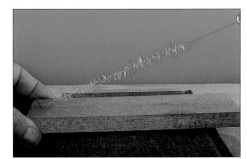

Step 3. Use Steps 4-5 of the **dubbing brush** method to finish the chenille. You can trim the chenille to the desired length at this time or trim it after it has been wrapped on the fly.

FEATHER BODIES

Wrapped feathers or herls (which are barbs) produce very lifelike bodies on nymph patterns. The following are a few basic methods for handling feathers and producing good durable bodies.

Wrapped Feather Bodies

Marabou and CDC feathers can be used to form bodies for nymph patterns. The feather can be wrapped on flat, to produce a thin body, or twisted and wrapped, to form a thicker, fuzzy body.

Flat-wrapped Feather Body

Step 1. Choose a feather whose barbs are aligned when preened toward the feather tip. A CDC feather is shown here. This type of feather will give you the most material to wrap the body.

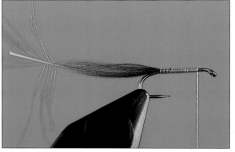

Step 2. Position the thread at the rear tie-in position. Use the **slide mount** method (p. 18) to mount the preened feather tip at the tie-in position. Then advance the thread to the front tie-off position.

Step 3. Preen any short barbs back down the stem. Wrap the feather forward with close or wide wraps to produce the body shape desired. Then secure the feather and trim the excess. These bodies should be counter-ribbed with fine wire for added strength.

Twisted Feather Body

A twisted feather body produces a chenille-like cord, which is stronger and bulkier than a flat-wrapped feather body. But twisting the feather does shorten the length of useable material.

Step 1. Choose a feather, marabou is used here, and prepare it as shown in Step 1 of the previous method. Use the **slide mount** method (p. 18) to mount the preened feather tip at the tie-position, with the tips extending back the desired length for the tail.

Step 2. Advance the thread to the forward tie-off position. Grip the butt end of the feather (with short feathers, use hackle pliers) and take a few clockwise twists, just enough to consolidate the barbs close to the hook shank.

Step 3. Wrap the feather forward. After every wrap or two, pause and twist the feather to consolidate the barbs. Continue until the body is wrapped; then secure the feather and trim the excess.

HERL BODIES

Peacock and marabou herls (barbs) are often used to form the bodies of nymphs. On smaller flies, a single strand of peacock can be wrapped to form the body, but often more than one strand is required to finish the body. In either case, the fragile herl should be ribbed to keep it from breaking. If you try to wrap a group of herls together, frequently a few of them will break before you complete the body. By twisting a core of thread or any other soft, stranded material together with the herls, you can produce a durable, dense chenille, that will not break when wrapped and does not need to be ribbed unless you desire it.

Following are two techniques for adding a core to herl. The first is the core-twisted herl method in which a single strand of material is used to reinforce the 2-4 herls. The second method is the loop-twisted herl in which a loop of material is used as a core for 5 or more herls. It should be noted that the barbules on the butt ends of the herls are less dense than those nearer the tip. As you approach the end of the twisted strands, the density of the barbules decreases, and it is best to tie them off and start a new bunch of herls.

E-Z Hook hackle pliers are employed in both methods here, but any hackle pliers can be used. If the pliers are not easy to spin, catch the finger loop of the pliers with a dubbing hook and spin its handle.

Core-twisted Herl Body

With this method, a single strand of material forms the core for twisting 2-4 herl strands, producing a strong, dense, chenille-like cord. If the body is formed first, the tag end of the tie-in thread can be used as the core material.

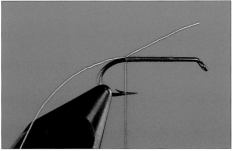

Step 1. Wrap the thread to the rear tie-in position. Use one thread wrap to mount a 6-inch strand of thread at the tie-in position. White thread is used here to show the strand; normally you would use a thread color that matches the color of the herl.

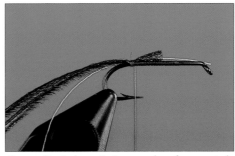

Step 2. Select 2-4 strands of material; three strands of peacock herl are used here. Align the strands and trim off the fragile tips. Mount the strands as a group at the tie-in position, directly over the thread strand. Secure them with 3-4 thread wraps.

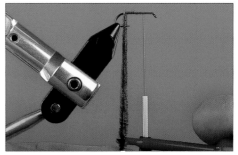

Step 3. Trim the excess herl and thread. Then form an even underbody as you wrap the thread to the forward tie-off position. Draw the herls and thread together under gentle even pressure. With hackle pliers grip the strands above your fingers.

Step 4. Even when using thread core you can break the herls by over-twisting them; so spin the hackle pliers clockwise just until the strands within an inch or so of the hook twist together into a chenille-like cord.

Step 5. Wrap the strands forward with close tight wraps; after each wrap, preen back the barbules to avoid trapping them. Continue wrapping the strands until you reach the end of the tightly twisted portion.

Step 6. Again twist the strands an inch or so down from the hook shank into a chenille-like cord and continue wrapping the body. On larger-bodied flies you may need to tie in additional sets of strands to complete the fly.

Loop-twisted Herl Body

Use this method when 5 or more herl strands need to be spun into a cord. Peacock herl is used here, but this technique works just as well with ostrich herl or marabou barbs.

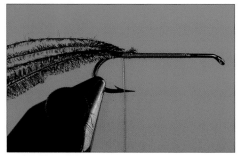

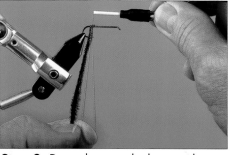

Step 1. Wrap the thread to the rear tie-in position. Select 5 or more herl strands, align them, and trim back the tips. Mount them as a group by their tips and trim the excess. Position the hanging thread 3 wraps forward from the rearmost thread wraps.

Step 2. Draw the strands down with your left thumb and forefinger, and hold them close to their ends. Form a loop by wrapping the thread around the tip of the forefinger, and return the thread to the hook shank, placing it over the hanging thread.

Step 3. Wrap the thread forward to the front tie-off position. Using E-Z Hook hackle pliers, grip the bottom of the thread loop and herl strands together. Then follow Steps 4-6 of the previous method to form the body.

RIBBING

Ribbing is used to accent a fly, either through flash or segmentation, and it can also be used to reinforce the body of the fly. This simple technique can make an ordinary fly body more durable, flashy, or lifelike. Wire, Mylar tinsel, and plastic ribbing are the materials most commonly used, but almost any thin-stranded material can be used to rib a fly. Ribbing wrapped in the same direction as the body wraps is the technique most often used by tiers. If the ribbing seems to get lost between the body segments or you wish to use ribbing to strengthen the body, then the counter-ribbing method should be used. There is no standard for the number of wraps used to rib a fly body. It's a personal choice, though it is common to use more wraps when reinforcing the body material.

Ribbing

With this technique, the ribbing material is wrapped in the same direction in which the body material was wrapped.

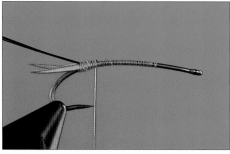

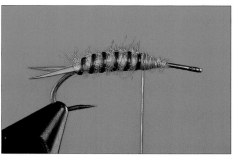

Step 1. Mount the tail. Mount the ribbing material directly on top of the rearmost thread wrap. Trim the excess.

Step 2. Dress the body; make sure the rearmost thread wraps are covered. With consistent tension on the ribbing material, wrap it forward in evenly spaced wraps.

Step 3. Wrap the ribbing to the tie-off position, secure the material, and trim the excess.

Counter-ribbing

With this method, the ribbing is wrapped in the opposite direction of the body material.

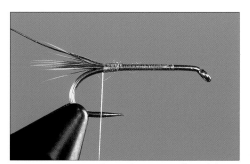

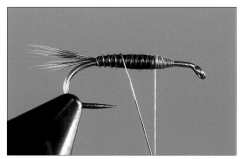

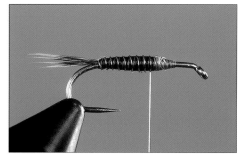

Step 1. Mount the tail. Mount the ribbing material on top of the rearmost thread wraps. Trim the excess.

Step 2. Dress the body. Using consistent tension and evenly spaced turns, wrap the ribbing material forward in the direction opposite that of the body wraps.

Step 3. Wrap the ribbing to the forward tie-off position. Secure it and trim the excess.

GILLS

On some nymphs and larvae, gills are very noticeable both to anglers and trout. Soft feather tufts, afterfeather, ostrich herl, and Antron yarn are the materials most commonly used to imitate gills. The following are a few basic methods of mounting gills on larva bodies. If you want to add tufted gills to a fly, use the **side-lashed bundled-fiber legs** method (p. 37) to mount them. To form lashed gills from an afterfeather, see Gilled Mayfly Nymph (p. 105).

Ribbed Gills

This technique is similar to ribbing the body; the ribbing material is wrapped in the same direction as the body wraps. Ribbed gills can be wrapped over any body, but they work best with segmented bodies, where the often fragile gill material can be wrapped between the segments to protect it from the sharp teeth of trout. Ostrich herl and Antron dubbing brushes work very well with this method. Ostrich herl can be wrapped by itself or reinforced with a thread core as shown here.

Step 1. Use one thread wrap to mount a 6-inch length of white 8/0 thread at the rear tie-in position. Align 1-3 white ostrich herls; remove their fragile tips, and use 3 thread wraps to mount them directly over the white thread. Trim the excess.

Step 2. Dress a segmented body. Micro Chenille is used here. Draw the herls and thread downward and grasp them with hackle pliers above your fingers as shown.

Step 3. With very little tension on the herls and thread, twist them clockwise into chenille. Do not over-twist or the herls will break.

Step 4. Wrap the twisted herl forward placing it between the wraps of the body material. Secure the herl at the front tie-off position and trim the excess.

Step 5. If an Antron **yarn dubbing brush** (p. 31) is used as the ribbing material, mount it at the rear tie-in position. Dress the body and wrap the material between the body segments.

Step 6. Secure the brush and trim the excess. If the fibers of the Antron brush are too long, trim them to the desired length at this time.

Bottom Lashed Gills

This method is used to imitate the gills that are found on some caddis larvae, but it can also be used to imitate the legs on a scud pattern. Ostrich herl is used with this method.

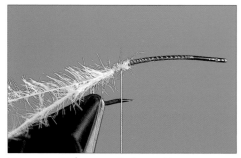

Step 1. At the rear tie-in position, mount a 4-in length of 2-pound mono on the bottom of the hook shank. Then align and trim the tips from 2-4 ostrich herls, and mount them on the bottom of the hook shank over the mono. Trim the excess.

Step 2. Mount a length of wire at the rear tie-in position and trim the excess. Dress the body. Gather the herl and mono; grasp their aligned ends with hackle pliers and twist them into a chenille-like cord. Do not overtwist the herls or they may break.

Step 3. Pull the herls forward and use 2 light thread wraps to secure them on the bottom at the front tie-in position. Wrap the wire rib forward and secure it at the tie-off position. Trim the excess wire and herl.

LEGS

Legs give a sunken fly a realistic appearance, and if made with a flexible material, they will also have a lifelike movement. Legs can be made of almost any suitably sized material. Feather barbs and rubber leg material are often used for legs on nymph and larva patterns. On smaller flies, the dubbing on the bottom of the thorax is often picked out to represent legs. The following methods can be adapted to mount the leg material of your choice. To form drawn feather legs, see Gilled Mayfly Nymph (p. 105).

Straight-lashed Legs

These legs are lashed across the hook shank before the body is dressed. For this method, the leg material must have a long uniform diameter. Rubber and latex strands, micro flocked yarn, and monofilament are good materials to use with this technique.

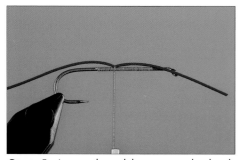

Step 1. Lay a thread base over the hook shank and hang the bobbin at the mounting position for the rear legs. Cut 3 equal lengths of rubber strands 2-3 inches long. Center one over the mounting position as shown. Secure it with 2 loose thread wraps.

Step 2. Use your fingers to turn the material perpendicular to the hook shank.

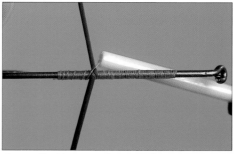

Step 3. Using tight-to-moderate tension, bring the tying thread up behind the near leg, cross the original mounting wraps, and then down in front of the far leg. Repeat this crossing wrap one more time to secure the material.

Step 4. At this time check the mounting of the material. If it is loose or out of position add a few more crisscross thread wraps to secure and align it. Advance the thread to the mounting position for the middle legs.

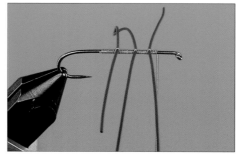

Step 5. Repeat Steps 1-4 to mount the middle legs. Advance the thread to the mounting position for the front legs. Repeat Steps 1-4 to mount the front legs.

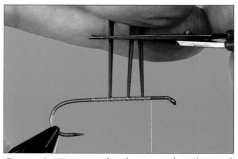

Step 6. To trim the legs to the desired length, pinch them between your left fingers, lift them above the hook shank as shown, and clip them parallel to the hook shank. To help secure the legs apply a drop of CA glue to the thread wraps.

Side-lashed Single-fiber Legs

With this technique, a single strand of material is mounted on the each side of the hook shank or to the side of the body. This method is demonstrated using goose biots in Steps 1-3. For multiple legs, repeat Steps 1-3 at each leg position. If a uniform-diameter material is used for the legs, a front pair of legs can be added to the body. This approach is shown in Steps 4-6.

Step 1. Dress the body. Form a tight thread base at the leg-mounting position. Place the leg material on the near side, with the desired length extending behind the hanging thread. Use the **soft wrap** method (p. 17) to secure it with 2 thread wraps.

Step 2. Make any adjustments to the leg at this time. Then repeat Step 1 to mount the far side leg.

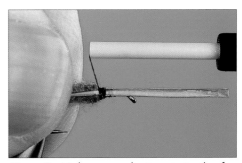

Step 3. Make any adjustments to the far side leg at this time. Then pinch the legs against the body and wrap the thread rearward to the front of the body to secure the legs.

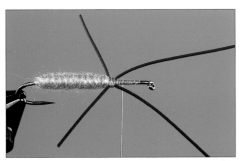

Step 4. To use a single stand of rubber for front and rear legs, follow the Steps 1-3 above and mount lengths of rubber to each side as shown. Fold the front legs back and advance the thread to the front leg position.

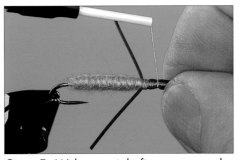

Step 5. With your right fingers, preen the front legs forward and pinch them against the hook shank in front of the hanging thread. With the bobbin in your left hand take 2 thread wraps to secure the legs.

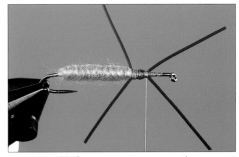

Step 6. Make any necessary adjustments to the front legs. Then take 2-3 more tight thread wraps over the mounting wraps. The legs can be trimmed to length at this time or after the fly is completed.

Side-lashed Bundled-fiber Legs

This technique is similar to the previous method, Steps 1-3, except that more care must be used in the placement of the aligned bundled materials. Once the bundle is mounted, it is difficult to make adjustments without throwing the fibers out of alignment. Any soft-fibered material can be used for legs in this method; aligned feather barbs are used most often.

Step 1. Dress the body. Form a tight thread base at the leg-mounting position. **Align and cut** (p. 22) the desired number of barbs from a feather. Use your right fingers to position the material at the desired length and angle on the near side.

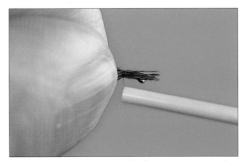

Step 2. With your left fingers, pinch the material tightly against the body, directly behind the hanging thread. Take one thread wrap around the body, and tighten the thread by pulling the bobbin directly toward you. Take 2 wraps in front of the first.

Step 3. With an equal-sized bundle of fibers, repeat Steps 1-2 on the far side of the hook shank. Trim the excess. To decrease the outward flare of the legs, pinch them against the body and take a few wraps rearward over the fibers.

Bundled-fiber Throat Legs

This widely-used method is also known as a throat hackle, but since it is most often used to represent legs and is similar to the side-lashed bundle-fiber method, I grouped it with the leg methods. Any soft-fibered material can be used, with feather barbs being the most common material. The fibers are normally placed at the front of the fly between the thorax and head.

Step 1. Dress the fly. Hang the thread at the mounting position. **Align and cut** (p. 22) the desired number of feather barbs. With your right fingers, position the fibers below the hook shank with the desired length extending behind the hanging thread.

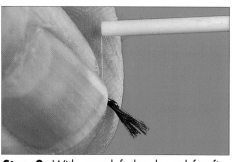

Step 2. With your left thumb and forefinger pinch the material directly over the hanging thread. Then using the **pinch wrap** method (p. 18) take 2 tight thread wraps to secure the bundle of fibers to the hook shank.

Step 3. Slight adjustment to the fibers can be made at this time. Then wrap the thread rearward to the body, and tighten each wrap by pulling directly upward. Trim the excess fibers.

WING CASES

As a nymph matures, its wing case becomes more pronounced and darkens as the enclosed wings develop. There are a large number methods and materials used to imitate these wing cases. With slight variations, these methods should enable you to form a wing cases for most nymph patterns. Wing cases are normally made from whole feathers, sections of feathers, or any suitable sheet material. These materials are often cut or burned to the desired shape. Whenever feathers are used for wing cases, it is best to reinforce them with a coat of flexible cement, like Flexament.

Folded Wing Case

This is probably the method most commonly used to form wing cases. Basically a strip of material or bundled of fibers is used to cover the thorax area. Though there are many variations of this method, all of them start with the basic technique shown below in Steps 1-6, where pheasant tail barbs are used. Turkey feather section is used in Steps 7-9 to show how the wing case can also be used to form the head of the fly.

Step 1. Complete the fly up to the rear of the thorax, and leave the thread hanging there. Cut a section of material as wide as the gap of the hook.

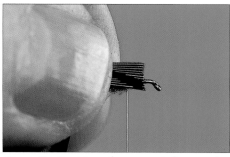

Step 2. Position the material over the abdomen with the butt ends facing forward over the tie-in position. The side you want facing upward on the finished wing case must be facing downward now.

Step 3. While holding the barbs firmly in place, secure them to the hook shank. Then wrap the thread rearward, stopping after binding the wing case atop the front of the abdomen with a few thread wraps, as shown.

Step 4. Dress the thorax, stopping 5-6 thread wraps behind the hook eye.

Step 5. With the right fingers, fold the wing case forward so that it smoothly covers the thorax. While holding the material in front of the hook eye, take 3 tight thread wraps over the material with your left hand.

Step 6. Trim the excess material and bind down the tag ends as you form the head.

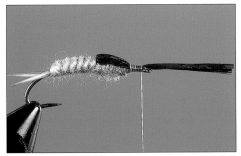

Step 7. To use the wing case to form the head of the fly, complete the fly as shown in Steps 1-5, except in Step 4 finish the thorax about 10 thread wraps behind the hook eye, as shown. Bind the wing-case tag ends to the hook shank up to the hook eye.

Step 8. Dub the head area, and leave the thread hanging in front of the thorax. Fold the wing-case material toward the rear with your left hand. Take 2 tight thread wraps to secure the material.

Step 9. Place 3 half-hitches directly over the thread wraps. Cut the thread and cement the thread wraps. Trim the butt end of the wing-case material to the desired length.

Cut Wing Cases

If a more realistic wing case is desired, the material can be cut to shape before it is mounted. Feathers, sections of feathers, and sheet materials can be used for this method. When feathers or sections of feathers are used, they should be coated with flexible cement, left to dry, and then cut to shape.

Step 1. Wing cases are normally about the width of the hook gap. Use the hook gap to measure the width, then push the point of it into the feather as shown. Slide the hook along the barb to separate the section. Cut the barbs close to the stem.

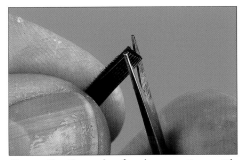

Step 2. Coat the feather section with Flexament and let it dry. Take the section and fold it in half lengthwise. Cut from the hinge of the fold up to the corners. How deep down the fold the cut is made will determine the angle of the wings.

Step 3. Unfold the cut wing case.

Burned Wing Cases

There are commercially made wing-case burners that can be used to produce very lifelike wing cases. Webby feathers from hen or game birds are used with this method.

Step 1. Select a feather that is large enough to form the wing case. Strip the lower fibers from the feather. Center the feather on the wing burner—low enough to get sufficient width, but high enough for sufficient length to mount the wing case.

Step 2. Pinch the feather into the wing burner, so that it is in the same position as shown in Step 1. Place the edge of the burner along side of the flame from a butane lighter, and burn away the excess feather barbs.

Step 3. Remove the feather from the burner, and use your finger to brush off the singed edges. To reinforce the feather, coat it with Flexament and let it dry before mounting it.

Mounting Cut or Burned Wing Cases

The following steps show how to mount one wing case, if more than one wing case is desired, repeat the steps for each wing case. It should be noted that no nymph has more than two wing cases. The most import part of this technique is to keep the wing case from flaring. This is accomplished by having a firm mounting base that is close to the final size or diameter of the finished body.

Step 1. Dress the body up to the wing-case mounting position. The body at this position must be firm and close to its final diameter. With your right hand, place the wing case over the mounting position.

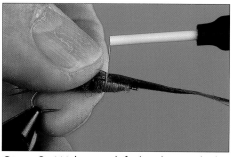

Step 2. With your left thumb, pinch the wing case in the mounting position, and secure it with 3 tight thread wraps.

Step 3. Trim the excess and bind down the butt ends.

WINGS

On subsurface flies, long wings that lay on top of the body are often called "down wings"; they are used to imitate wings on sunken adult insects. Short wings placed on the back or sides of the fly are normally used to imitate wings on emerging insects. There are a large number of materials that can be used for making wings. Durability, buoyancy, softness, looks, and ease of handling, are characteristics to keep in mind, whether choosing natural or synthetic materials. The following methods can be adapted to form most wings used on sunken flies.

Feather-Tip Emerger Wings—Top Mounted

Shown in the following steps, feather-tip wings can be mounted on the top of the body to imitate wings on an emerging mayfly. They can also be mounted on the sides of the body to imitat caddis pupae as shown in the following Burned Feather Wings method. Matching hen feathers are used in this demonstration but any suitable feather may be used. You can place the feathers convex sides together, so they flare apart as shown here, or you can place the concave sides together to form a single flat wing.

Step 1. Dress the fly to the wing mounting position. Select two feathers and strip the fluff from them. With your right fingers, hold the convex sides together with the tips aligned. Place them over the mounting position to give the desired length.

Step 2. With your left fingers, pinch the feather at the mounting position and used the **pinch wrap** method (p. 18) to mount the feathers with 3 thread wraps.

Step 3. Slight adjustments can be made to the feathers at this time. After the feathers are adjusted, pinch them behind the mounting wraps and take 2 more thread wraps to secure the feathers. Trim the excess.

Burned Feather Emerger Wings—Side Mounted

Realistic caddis pupae wings can be formed with a wing burner. These wings are mounted on the sides of the fly. Feather-tip or cut-feather wings can also be mounted using this method. To keep side-mounted wings from flaring out when mounted, the mounting position should be firm and close to the same diameter of the body. To make the wings more durable, coat them with Flexament before or after mounting them.

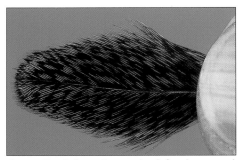

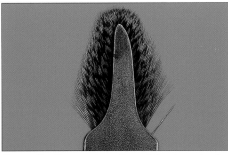

Step 1. Select 2 matched feathers and strip away the lower barbs. Place the concave sides of the feathers together, and align the tips and stems.

Step 2. Center the aligned feathers in the wing burner. A small mayfly wing burner is used here.

Step 3. Hold the wing burner alongside the edge of the flame from a butane lighter, and burn off the exposed barbs.

Step 4. Remove the feathers from the burner and brush the soot from the edges. With your right fingers place one feather, extended to the desired length and with the concave side facing in, at the wing mounting position on the near side of the fly.

Step 5. With your left fingers, pinch the feather at the mounting position and take 3 thread wraps to mount the feather.

Step 6. Remove your fingers and check the position of the wing; slight adjustments can be made at this time. Repeat Steps 4-5 to mount the feather on the far side and trim the excess.

Folded Cut Emerger Wings

These wings are made from a single piece of folded material that is cut to shape and mounted over the top of the body. Feathers or sections of feather that have been coated with Flexament or thin sheet-wing material can be used to form these wings. Folded wings are normally used on caddis pupae patterns.

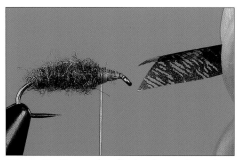 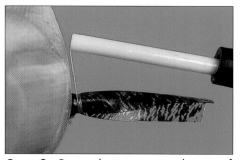 

Step 1. Dress the fly body to the wing-mounting position. Select a material; Thin Skin is used here. Cut a strip that is about twice as wide as the hook gap, fold it in half, and cut it at the angle shown.

Step 2. Center the wings over the top of the body at tie-in position, extending them rearward to the desired length. While holding the wings with your left fingers, mount them with 3-4 tight thread wraps.

Step 3. Slight adjustments can be made at this time. If the wings are flared, take a few thread wraps toward the hook bend to reduce the flare. Trim the excess and bind down the butt end.

Preparing Quill Wings

Quill downwings or emerger wings are made from feather sections cut from a matching pair of duck flight feathers. The thick, spongy barbs forming the tip sections of flight feathers are not suitable for forming wings; cut the wings from lower sections of the feathers where the barbs are more uniform. Most downwings are formed with feather sections that are as wide as the hook gap, using the hook as a measuring gauge, as shown below.

Step 1. To separate the desired width of barbs from the feather, use the hook gap as the measuring gauge. Place the hook at the midpoint of the barbs, with the shank against edge of the barbs, and then insert the hook point into the barbs, as shown.

Step 2. Slide the hook point along the length of the barb to separate the section from the upper feather.

Step 3. Cut the section from the feather. Repeat Steps 1-3 to cut a feather section from same area on the matching feather. The matched wings are now ready for mounting.

Paired Quill Downwings

With this wing method, a matching pair of quill sections are mounted on top of the hook shank. The feather sections can be mounted with their concave sides facing outward, producing divided wings, or as shown in the following steps, with the concave sides facing one another, producing a flat single wing. Having the pointed ends of the feather sections turned upward is the traditional mounting position of the wings, as shown below, but downward-facing tips are often used to imitate wings on sunken adult caddis patterns.

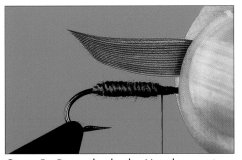

Step 1. Dress the body. Use the previous method to form a matched pair of wings and align them with their concave sides together. With your right fingers, position the wings over body, extending the desired length behind the hanging thread as shown.

Step 2. With your left fingers, tightly pinch the wings directly over the mounting position. Use the **pinch wrap** method (p. 18) to mount the wings to the hook shank.

Step 3. The wings should appear as a flat panel. Trim the excess and bind down the butt ends.

Quill Emerger Wings

These emerger wings are made from matching feather sections that are mounted to the sides of the hook shank. The tips of the feather sections can be mounted upward with the concave side of the wings facing outward to imitate emerging mayfly wings, or as shown below, with the tips pointed downward with the concave sides of the wings facing inward to imitate caddis emerger wings. To make the wings more durable, coat them with Flexament and let them dry before mounting them.

Step 1. Dress the body. Use the **preparing quill wings** (p. 44) method to form wings that are about half the width of the hook gap. With your right fingers, place the nearside wing, with the concave side facing inward, at the desired position.

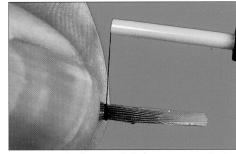

Step 2. With your left fingers, pinch the wing against the body behind the hanging thread. Take two loose thread wraps to hold the feather in position.

Step 3. Remove your fingers and check the position of the wing. Make any necessary adjustments at this time.

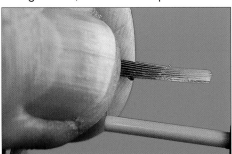

Step 4. Place your fingers over the thread wraps; firmly pinch the wing against the hook shank and tighten the thread wraps.

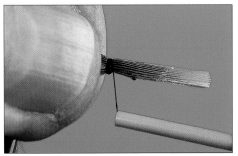

Step 5. Slide your fingers back to expose the thread wraps and take 2 more tight wraps to secure the wing.

Step 6. Mount the far wing by repeating Steps 1-5. Trim the butt ends and bind them down with additional thread wraps.

Bundled-fiber Downwings

Aligned hair, feather barbs, and synthetic fibers can be used to form wings that are mounted atop of the hook shank. These wings may not produce the clean silhouette of quill wings, but they are easier to mount and are more durable. The amount of material used to make the wing should be no more than the outside diameter of the hook eye when the material is twisted into a cord. For smaller bundles of material, use the **pinch wrap** method (p. 18) to mount them on top of the hook shank. With larger bundles or slippery materials, use the method shown below to consolidate the material on top of the hook shank.

 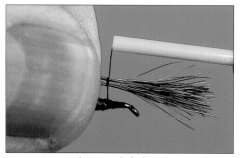 

Step 1. Dress the body. Use the one of the **preparing materials** methods (p. 22) to gather and align the tips; squirrel tail is used here. With your right fingers, position the bundle over the body, extending the wing to the desired length.

Step 2. With your left finger, pinch the bundle directly behind the mounting point. Take a turn of thread around the bundle as shown.

Step 3. With light tension on the thread, roll or slip the bundle down to the hook shank. While holding the bundle in position, take 4-6 very tight thread wraps to secure the wing. Trim the excess and bind down the butt ends.

Cut Antron Wing Buds

Antron yarn or any other suitable material can be used with this method to make emerger wings. A thick wing is not needed; use just enough material to form a thin wing. These durable wings are easy to mount and shape.

Step 1. Dress the body, tapering the front. Center a 2-3 inch length of Antron yarn in front of the body, and secure it with 2 thread wraps.

Step 2. Pull the near side strand toward the rear, and angle it downward. Take 2-3 thread wraps to secure the wing over the tapered end of the body as shown.

Step 3. Repeat Step 2 to mount the far side wing. Trim the wings at the desired length and angle. Cement the mounting thread wraps to keep them from slipping.

Looped Antron Wing Buds

With this method, Antron yarn or any other suitable material is used to form wing buds that are mounted to the sides of the body.

Step 1. Dress the body, tapering the front. Center and mount a thin 3-inch strand of Antron yarn in front of the body. Fold the near strand rearward and downward. Use 2 thread wraps to secure it to the side of the body as shown.

Step 2. Fold the near strand forward, placing it above the lower strand to form a small loop. Use 2 thread wraps to secure the strand to the body as shown. Slight adjustments can be made to the loop at this time.

Step 3. Repeat Step 1-2 to form the loop wing on the far side. Trim the excess and bind down the butt ends. Cement the thread-mounting wraps to keep them from slipping.

HACKLE

Dry-fly hackle gets the most attention from fly tiers, and many believe that any unusable dry-fly hackle will make a good wet-fly hackle. Most of the time this is not the case. It is best to choose hackle feathers used on sunken flies for properties that will enhance the looks of the fly, give the fly the proper silhouette in the legs or body, and have a thin stem for easy wrapping.

Almost any thin-stemmed feather can be used as a collar hackle on wet flies, since most require only a few wraps of the feather. Feathers with webby, soft barbs make the best wet-fly collar hackles. These feathers are normally found on body, saddle, and neck feathers from hens and game birds.

For wet flies, a long webby feather with a thin stem is needed to palmer hackle over a body. Two or three feathers can be used to palmer hackle over a fly body, but a single long hackle is more aesthetically pleasing and easier to wrap. These long feathers are normally found on rooster or hen saddles.

Not all wet-fly hackle is formed from wrapped feathers. Fibers from feathers, fur, yarn, or any other fine-fibered material can be spun around the hook shank to form the hackle (see **bundle-fiber throat legs** p. 38). Or fibers can be inserted into a thread or wire loop, spun into a chenille and wrapped.

The following methods should enable you to hackle most nymph, pupa, and wet-fly patterns.

SIZING HACKLE FEATHERS

For wet flies, the size of the hackle is determined by its function on the finished fly. When the hackle is used to imitate the legs on nymph and pupa patterns, the barbs should approximate the length of the legs on the natural insect. If the hackle is used to shape the body or to give the impression of body movement, then choose feathers with soft, long barbs that will cover the intended part of the fly.

As you can see, there is no set rule for hackle size on sunken flies. Fly pattern recipes may tell what size hackle to use, often using the hook gap as the reference gauge. Most fly-pattern books have photos of the fly patterns; if the recipe does not give the hackle size, then try to gauge the hackle size from the photo.

Sizing a hackle to look proportional is often a trial-and-error process. To find the appropriate hackle size, choose a feather and bend it over the part of the fly where it is to be wrapped; continue testing feathers until you find the hackle length desired. With longer feathers, this gauging can be done with the feathers still attached to the skin. Smaller feathers must be removed from the skin to check their hackle length.

Sizing a Hackle

To check the hackle length, fold the feather over the part of the fly where it will be wrapped. Choose a feather with the desired barb length.

Preparing Hackle Feathers for Mounting

Wet-fly hackle feathers can be mounted on the hook shank by either the stem or the tip. Shown here are two ways to prepare the feathers for mounting.

Preparing Stem-mount Feathers

Unless the pattern calls for using the fuzzy barbs, strip the lower barbs from the feather until you reach a point where the stem is thin enough to wrap.

Preparing Tip-mount Feathers

At the feather tip, use your left fingers to pinch the barbs that are too short to wrap. With your right fingers, preen the lower barbs down until they are perpendicular to the stem.

Mounting Collar Hackle Feathers

There are a number of ways to mount collar hackle feathers. Shown below are two popular methods for mounting feathers either by the stem or tip. For wet flies, the feather is normally mounted so that when it is lifted perpendicularly to begin the wraps, the convex or front side of the feather will be facing the hook eye. This will cause the hackle tips to angle toward the hook bend as the feather is wrapped. If you want a hackle that stands perpendicular to the hook shank, mount the feather so that the concave or back side of the feather faces the hook eye.

Steps 1-2 show mounting a feather by the tip before the body is dressed; the feather can also be mounted by the stem. Whether the feather is mounted by the tip or stem, on smaller flies the technique shown here will reduce the bulk in the head area, making small neat heads possible.

Step 3 shows the feather mounted by its stem after the body has been dressed. This mounting technique can be used on flies when extra bulk in the head area is not an issue. A feather can also be mounted by the tip using this method. In fact, feathers with thick stems at their base should be mounted by their tips.

Step 1. Lay a thread base over the mounting area, and leave the hanging thread at the mounting position. Prepare a feather for tip-mounting as shown above. With the front of the feather facing down, mount the tip at the tie-in position as shown.

Step 2. Trim the excess feather, and bind down the ends. Dress the body up to the hackle-mounting position, and wrap the thread forward to the hook eye. Pull the hackle upward; it is now ready to be wrapped.

Step 3. Dress the body, leaving the thread in front of the body. Prepare a feather for stem mounting as shown above. With the convex or front side of feather facing upward, mount it at the tie-in position. Trim the excess stem.

Wet-Fly Collar Hackle—Stem Mounted

This method works best with uniform, thin-stemmed feathers. Wet-fly collar hackles are mounted in front of the body, and the feather is normally wrapped forward with close tight wraps until the desired amount of hackle is applied.

Step 1. Prepare and mount a feather by its stem as shown above. Grasp the tip of the feather with hackle pliers, and using close, tight wraps, take the desired number of turns forward.

Step 2. While maintaining tension on the hackle, take the bobbin in your left hand and secure the feather with 3 tight wraps.

Step 3. Trim the excess and bind down the tag ends.

Wet-Fly Collar Hackle—Tip Mounted

This technique can be used with any feather but is best suited for feathers with an extreme taper or with thick-butted stems. When a tapered feather is mounted by its tip, and wrapped forward, the longest barbs will be at the front of the hackle. A feather with a thick stem should be mounted by the tip to reduce the bulk in the hackle area and to form close, tight hackle wraps.

Step 1. Using one of the **mounting collar hackle feather** techniques shown above, mount a feather by the tip. Grip the stem of the feather with hackle pliers, and using close, firm wraps, take the desired number of turns forward.

Step 2. While maintaining tension on the feather, use your left hand to take 3 tight thread wraps to secure the feather.

Step 3. Trim the excess feather and bind down the tag end.

Folded Collar Hackle

When feathers refuse to angle back toward the rear of the hook because of thick or thin stems, folding the hackle back while it is being wrapped will often produce the desired slant. If the barbs need to be slanted more toward the rear, Steps 5-6 can be used.

Step 1. Mount a feather in front of the body as shown in **mounting collar hackle feathers** (p. 46). Grip the feather with hackle pliers, raise the feather, and use your left fingers to preen the barbs back as shown.

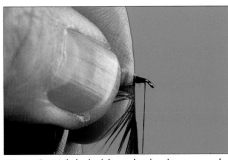

Step 2. While holding the barbs, wrap the hackle. Release the barbs as the hackle is wrapped beneath the shank. When the feather clears the bottom of the hook, preen the barb back as shown and continue wrapping the feather.

Step 3. Repeat Steps 1-2, preening the barbs back until the desired number of wraps are taken. With your left hand holding the bobbin, take 3 tight thread wraps to secure the feather.

Step 4. Trim the excess and bind down the tag end. Leave the thread hanging in front of the hackle.

Step 5. If more of a slant is desired on the barbs, use your left fingers to preen the hackle barbs back. While holding them in position, take a few thread wraps over the frontmost hackle barbs to force them toward the rear.

Step 6. Remove your fingers; if more hackle slant is needed repeat Step 5. When the desired slant is achieved, complete the fly.

Forward Palmer Hackle—Stem Mounted

This body-hackle method is best suited to long feathers with barbs of consistent length. When wrapped, these feathers will produce a uniformly spreading hackle along the body. Hackle on a wet fly is normally mounted with the front of the feather facing the hook eye; when it is wrapped, the barbs will slant toward the rear. The number of wraps taken over a body can be dense or sparse, depending on the pattern. A wire **counter-wrapped rib** (p. 35) is often used to reinforce the hackle stem.

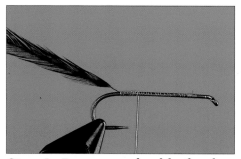

Step 1. Prepare a hackle feather for stem mounting (p. 45). Mount the feather at the rear tie-in position with the front of the feather facing forward. Leave a small amount of barbless stem above the thread wraps as shown.

Step 2. Dress the body, taking one wrap of the body material behind the feather. Leave the thread hanging in front of the body at the tie-off position.

Step 3. Grip the feather with hackle pliers and wrap the feather forward with evenly spaced wraps. Control the twist of the feather with the hackle pliers. Secure the feather at the tie-off position. Trim the excess and bind down the end.

Forward Palmer Hackle—Tip Mounted

Tapered feathers, where the base barbs are longer than the tip barbs, should be used with this method. When a tip-mounted feather is wrapped forward on the body, the shorter barbs will be at the rear of the body and the longest ones at the front, producing a tapered body hackle.

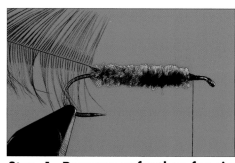

Step 1. Prepare a feather for tip mounting (p. 46), and mount it at the rear tie-in position. Dress the body, taking one wrap of the body material behind the feather. Leave the thread at the front of the body.

Step 2. Wrap the feather forward with evenly spaced wraps. With each wrap, preen the barbs toward the rear to keep them from being trapped under the next wrap.

Step 3. Continue wrapping to the front tie-off position. Secure the feather, trim the excess and bind down the ends.

Loop-Spun Collar Hackle

An effective collar hackle for wet flies can be produced from long-fibered furs, yarns, or any other suitable fibers, by using a dubbing loop to trap the material, which is then spun into a chenille and wrapped. Rabbit fur is used in the following steps. This method is easily adapted to form an Antron yarn hackle, just brush out a strand of yarn, cut the fibers to the desired length, and use it in place of the fur in the following steps.

Step 1. Position the thread at the hackle-mounting position. Form a **dubbing loop** (p. 28) and apply a light coat of dubbing wax to the loop.

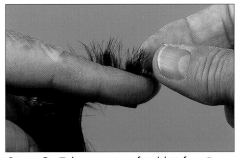

Step 2. Take a strip of rabbit fur; "scissors" about 1-2 inches between your left fingers and align the tips. While holding the tips, cut the fur close to the hide.

Step 3. Clean most of the underfur from the hair. Insert the hair into the loop, so it is uniformly distributed along the thread loop with the tips aligned. The distance the tips extend past the thread will be the length of the finished hackle.

Step 4. Catch the bottom of the loop with a dubbing hook, and pull down to close the loop. While maintaining tension on the loop, carefully trim the fur butts close to the thread.

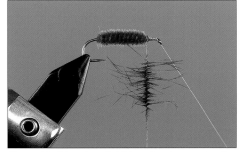

Step 5. Use the dubbing hook to spin the loop clockwise into a tight cord.

Step 6. Wrap the spun hair the desired number of turns, preening the fibers back after each wrap. Secure the loop with 3 tight thread wraps and trim the excess. Take a few thread wraps over the frontmost fibers to slant them back to the desired angle.

EYES

Eyes can be used to add a realistic touch to nymph patterns or to add extra weight to the front of the fly. The following methods show a few ways to produce eyes and how to mount them on the hook shank.

Making Mono Eyes

Pre-formed mono or plastic eyes are sold in most fly shops, and for patterns requiring large eyes these work very well. But when smaller eyes are needed, I like to make my own, and get a custom fit for the fly. On small flies, the spacing between the eyes is very important to the appearance of the finished fly. By making your own eyes, you can control the width of the gap and the size of the eye to match the fly you are tying. Both nylon and copolymer leader materials can be used to form the following eyes. It is important to use a pair of locking forceps or pliers with a tapered jaw to hold the mono. The mono is placed crosswise in the jaws, at the point where the width of the jaw is equal to the distance desired between the eyes. Then the eyes are formed by melting the mono to the desired size, with the largest practical maximum being about 2 times the diameter of the mono used. Use a long-neck butane lighter that has an adjustable flame, the type used to light barbecues. Melt the mono, but don't let it burn, it becomes too difficult to control the size of the eyes being formed.

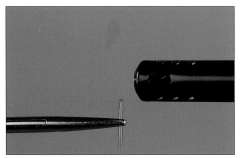

Step 1. Grasp a 1/2- to 1-inch length of mono crosswise in the pliers at a position in the jaws that is equal to the desired width between the eyes. Position the flame above the mono and slowly lower it until the mono starts to melt.

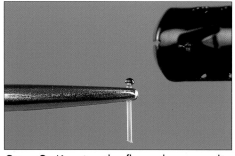

Step 2. Keeping the flame the same distance from the melting mono, follow it down until the melting ball reaches the pliers. Do not hurry; melt the mono slowly or it will start to burn. If it burns, blow out the flame and continue.

Step 3. Allow the melted eye to cool, turn the pliers over, and form the opposite eye.

Making Glass Bead Eyes

Melted mono can be used to form eyes from glass or metal beads. This method is useful for forming larger eyes than is possible by melting mono alone. Glass beads are most often used with this method, allowing you to choose the size and color. Metal beads can also be used when added weight is desired, but pre-made metal eyes are more durable and easier to secure to the hook shank. Use a thickness of mono that is close to the diameter of the bead opening. To melt the mono, follow the directions for forming the mono eyes shown in the previous method.

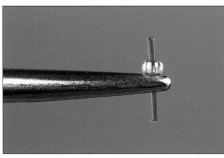

Step 1. Cut a 1/2- to 1-inch length of mono and place it crosswise in the pliers. Hold the mono vertically and slip a bead over the end.

Step 2. Melt the mono down to the glass bead, following the directions given in the previous method.

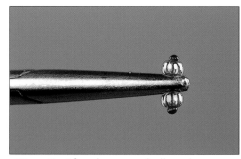

Step 3. After the mono ball cools, repeat Steps 1-2 to form the other eye.

Mounting Eyes

There are a number of ways to mount barbell eyes but the following method provides a very secure mount that will hold the eyes in position in all but the most extreme cases. When using heavy lead barbell eyes as shown below, you need to secure them firmly to the hook shank or they will loosen and ruin the fly. Heavy metal eyes that are mounted on top of the hook shank will cause the fly to turn over and ride hook point upward; this reduces snagging the fly while it is fished. If you want the fly to ride hook-point down, then mount the heavy metal eye on the bottom of the hook shank.

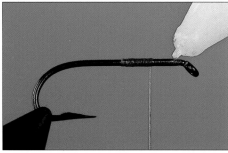

Step 1. Using close tight wraps, lay a thread base from the hook eye back to the middle of the hook shank; then return the thread to the mounting position. Coat the thread wraps with CA glue and let it dry.

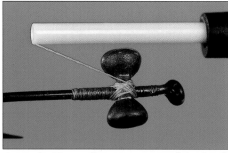

Step 2. Mount the eye on top of the hook shank using tight, crisscross thread wraps. Continue the wraps until the eyes are firmly mounted.

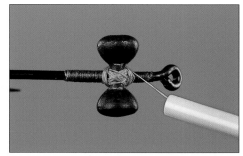

Step 3. To tighten the wraps more, take a number of tight wraps around the base of the eyes above the hook shank. The eye should now be locked in position. Coat the thread wraps with CA glue.

BEAD HEADS

Metal and glass beads can be used to add weight, flash, or color to the front of sunken flies. The following methods show how to mount these beads securely to the hook. Choose beads that do not require you to bend the hook. Opening the hook bend in order to slide on a bead can weaken or break the hook.

Metal Bead Heads

Metal beads for heads come in a number of different sizes; choose the size that matches the hook. Metal beads that have a uniform-diameter hole are difficult to slide on the shank without bending open the hook bend, unless the bead has a large-diameter hole. If you are using a bead with a uniform-diameter hole, mount it using the **glass bead-head** method that follows.

Metal beads that have counterdrilled or tapered holes will slide around the hook bend of most hooks. A counterdrilled bead is used in the following method, though the same mounting technique will work with tapered-hole beads.

Glass and metal beads can be difficult to handle, the last method shows how to alter a pair of X-ACTO self-closing tweezers into super-gripping bead tweezers.

Step 1. Insert the hook point into the smaller of the two holes, and slide the bead into position behind the hook eye.

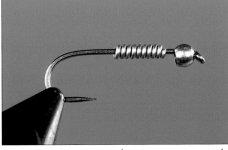

Step 2. Using wire that is approximately the same diameter of the hook shank, use the **direct wrap lead underbody** method (p. 20) to wrap the desired amount of wire onto the hook shank. You will need at least 4-5 wraps.

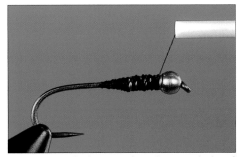

Step 3. Push the wire into the rear hole of the bead. This will center the bead on the hook shank and add weight to the front of the fly. Mount the thread behind the wire and form a tapered base at the rear to secure the wire; then wrap over the wire.

Glass Bead Heads

Glass beads form lighter heads and offer a wide range of color choices. Their main fault is that they can break while fishing. The following mounting method is used to hold the bead firmly in place, reducing the chances of breakage. This method can also be used to mount metal beads with holes of uniform diameter.

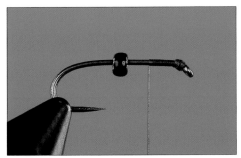

Step 1. Slide the bead onto the hook. Choose a color of thread that matches the bead and mount it directly behind the hook eye. Form a small thread bump behind the hook eye, and wrap a layer of thread 2 bead-widths rearward.

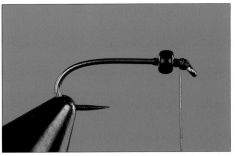

Step 2. Wrap the thread forward to the thread bump. Slide the bead forward onto the thread wraps; if it is loose, add more layers of thread until the bead will just slip over the thread wraps. Tie off the thread in front of the thread bump.

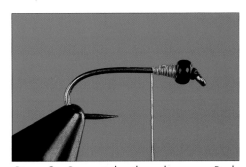

Step 3. Cement the thread wraps. Push the bead against the thread bump. Mount the tying thread behind the bead and build up a small thread bump against the back of the bead to secure it.

Bead Tweezers

You need a pair of self-closing tweezers, X-ACTO 4 1/2-inch #X73370 are shown here, available at hobby shops. Dave's Flexament is used for the coating; it will eventually wear off and not grip the beads; when this happens, peel off the old coating and apply a new coat of glue. Two to three coats are needed to form a good gripping surface; let each coat dry for 2-3 hours before adding another coat.

To pick up a bead so the hole is facing out from the jaws of the tweezers, place the beads on a flat surface, the beads will settle with their holes facing upward. Use the tweezers to grasp the bead by the side and the hole will be facing outward as shown in Step 3 below.

Step 1. Place a pencil or similar object between the jaws of the tweezers to hold them open. Use a fine metal file to rough up the surface of the tweezers, around both tips and about half an inch up the stems.

Step 2. Clean the tips with lacquer thinner. Dip the tip of the open tweezers into the Flexament. Rotate the tweezers to even out the glue. Hang the tweezers, with the tips pointing straight down, for 2-3 hours until the glue is dry.

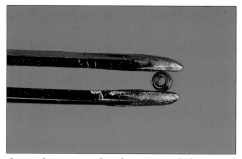

Step 3. Repeat the dipping and drying of the coats two or more times until a good coat of glue covers the tips. Place the bead on a flat surface; then use the tweezers to grasp the bead by the sides as shown.

NATURALS

When tying a nymph pattern that is supposed to imitate what the fish are feeding on, it helps to have an idea of what the natural looks like. The following photographs can be used as a guide to the shape, size, and color of various naturals in a trout's diet. You do not have to match the natural perfectly, but to get the trout's attention, you do need to produce a fly that at least resembles the appearance or behavior of the creature you are trying to imitate. The common names for most aquatic insects are descriptions of the adult form, so names like Blue-wing Olive may not make much sense when looking at the nymphal stage of the insect. Maybe some day, nymphs will have common names of their own, but until then we have to use the common name of the adults.

MAYFLY NYMPHS

Mayfly nymphs are divided into four groups, based on the behavior of the nymphs. The mayflies within each group normally have the similar body shapes, but sizes and color vary.

Mayfly Swimmer Nymphs: Common names are Blue-winged Olive, Speckle-winged Quill, and Black Drake. These nymphs have slender, tapered bodies, most with three fringed tails. They range from 4mm to 25mm in length.

Mayfly Crawler Nymphs: Common names are Hendrickson, Pale Morning Dun, Western Green Drake, Mahogany Duns, and Tricos. These nymphs have rather square heads and rectangular bodies with fine tails. They range from 4mm to 18mm in length.

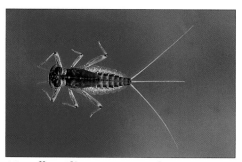

Mayfly Clinger Nymphs: Common names are Gordon Quill, Yellow Quill, Light Cahill, Pale Evening Dun, and March Brown. These nymphs have flattened bodies, with 2 or 3 tails. They range from 7mm to 16mm in length.

Mayfly Burrower Nymphs: Common names are Eastern Green Drake, Brown Drake, Big Yellow May, and White Mayfly. These nymphs have large bodies with large gills, and three fringed tails. They range from 12mm to 35mm in length.

STONEFLY NYMPHS

Stoneflies are separated into five basic groups. Golden Stoneflies and Giant Stoneflies are pictured separately. The remaining three, Little Brown Stoneflies, Little Yellow Stoneflies, and Little Green Stoneflies—Little Stoneflies—are shown here as one group.

Golden Stonefly Nymphs: Common names are Golden Stone, Brown Willow Fly, Great Stonefly. These nymphs have distinctive dark markings on their backs. They range from 25mm to 40mm in length and yellow to brown in color.

Giant Stoneflies: Common names are Giant Salmon Fly, Giant Black Stonefly, Small Salmon Fly. These nymphs have large round bodies with short tails. They range from 30mm to 60mm in length and are dark brown to black in color.

Little Stoneflies: Common names are Little Brown Stoneflies, Little Green Stoneflies, and Little Yellow Stoneflies. These small stoneflies vary in shape from round and slender to short and squat. They range from 6mm to 18mm in length and brown to yellow in color.

CADDIS LARVAE AND PUPAE

For the fly tier, caddis larvae are placed into three groups—free-living, net-spinning, and case-building. An example of each is shown. Since caddis pupae all have the same general shape, for fly-tying purposes they can be represented by a single example.

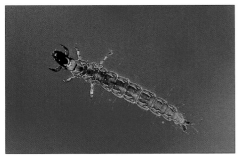

Fee-living Caddis Larvae: Its common name is Green Rock Worm. These larvae have long grub-like bodies with gills that are small or not visible at all. They range from 8mm to 20mm in length and green to brown in color.

Net-spinning Caddis Larvae: Common names are Spotted Sedge and Little Autumn Stream Sedge. They have grub-like bodies, often with noticeable gills along the bottom of the abdomen. They range from 8mm to 20mm in length and green to brown in color.

Stone-cased Caddis Larvae: Common name Fall Caddis. These larvae build stone cases that range from 25mm-40mm in length.

Tube-cased Caddis Larvae: Common names are American Grannom, Black Caddis, Mother's Day Caddis, and Traveling Sedge. These larvae build tapered rectangular or cylinder-shaped cases, ranging from 6mm-45mm in length.

Weed-cased Caddis Larvae: Common names are Cream Sedge and Cinnamon Caddis. These cases have a roughly cylindrical shape, that range from 15mm to 30mm in length.

Caddis Pupae: Common names, Caddis Pupa and Emergent Sedge. The overall body shape, folded wings, legs and antennae are similar on most caddis pupae. They range from 6mm-25mm in length and the colors vary from greens to browns.

MIDGE LARVAE AND PUPAE

Midges (or Chironomidae) are often thought of as being very small insects. This is true for most stream midges, but midges that live in stillwaters often get very large. Large or small, though, they are very important food sources for trout.

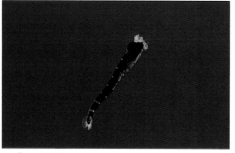

Lake Midge Larvae: Common names are Blood Worm and Midge Larva. These larvae have short worm-like bodies, ranging from 10mm to 20mm in length. Colors vary from reds, creams, browns, and greens to black.

Lake Midge Pupae: Common names are Buzzer Pupa and Midge Pupa. These pupae have tapered bodies, often with noticeable wings and with gills at both ends. They range from 8mm-20mm in length. Colors are black, browns, creams, greens, or reds.

River Midge Pupae: Common name Midge Pupa. These pupae have tapered bodies, with noticeable wings. They range from 2mm to 7mm in length. Colors vary—blacks, browns, greens, creams, or reds.

DRAGONFLY AND DAMSELFLY NYMPHS

These large nymphs occur most often in stillwaters and are readily taken by trout. For the fly tier, dragonfly nymphs can be placed in two groups based on their habits and shapes. Because most damselfly species share a similar profile and behavior they can be represented by a single example.

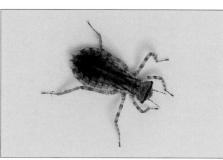

Climber Dragonfly Nymphs: Common names are Dragonfly Nymph, Blue Darner and Green Darner. Their bodies are long and cylindrical in shape, with large eyes. They range from 30mm to 50mm in length. Colors vary—browns, grays, or greens.

Sprawler Dragonfly Nymphs: Common names are Dragonfly Nymph and Skimmer. The bodies on these nymphs are broad and squat, with large eyes. They range from 20mm to 30mm in length. Colors vary from browns to greens.

Damselfly Nymphs: Common names are Damsels and Dancers. They have long slender bodies, with three tail-like gills and large eyes. They range from 15mm to 30mm in length. Colors vary from browns to greens.

MISCELLANEOUS

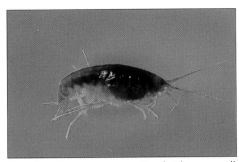

Scuds: Common name Scud. These small crustaceans are a very important food source for trout in both lakes and streams. They range from 5mm to 25mm in length. Colors vary from olive, to tan, to gray.

Aquatic Sowbugs: Common names are Sowbug and Cress Bug. These small crustaceans have flattened bodies. They range from 5mm to 20mm in length. Colors vary from browns to greens.

Water Boatmen: Common name Water Boatman. Their bodies have a flattened, oval shape, with pronounced swimming legs. They range from 6mm-12mm in length. Colors vary from browns, to greens.

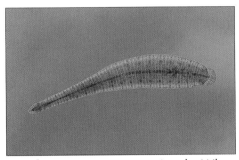

Leeches: Common name Leech. When swimming, the bodies extend to a long, slender shape. They range from 1mm to 40mm in length. Colors vary—blacks, browns, to olives.

Chapter 2

Lashed and Extended Bodies

Lashed-body and extended-body patterns are easy to tie, and with a few variations and some imagination you should be able to tie flies with this body style that will cover most of the major insect groups. Materials used for extended bodies should be flexible or they may interfere with the pattern's hooking ability.

Lashed and Extended Bodies—Ultra Chenille

San Juan Worm, Vernille

Originator: Chuck Rizuto
Hook: Scud, 2X wide, 2X heavy, sizes 12-14
Thread: Red 6/0 or color to match body
Weight: Optional, copper wire same color as body
Body: Red, maroon, tan, brown, or orange Vernille or Ultra Chenille

Beaded San Jan Worm

Hook: Scud, size 14
Thread: Tan, or color to match body
Bead: Brass bead, 3/32 two-diameter hole beads from Spirit River
Body: Tan Vernille or Ultra Chenille

Note: The San Juan Worm imitates aquatic earthworms found in most rivers. While an effective pattern on most rivers, it's often the go-to pattern on tailwater fisheries.

San Juan Worm, Red

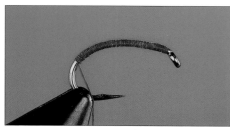

Step 1. Mount a nymph hook in the vise and tie in the thread just behind the hook eye. Using tight, close thread wraps, move the thread back to the position shown.

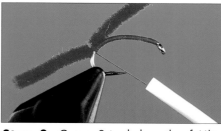

Step 2. Cut a 2-inch length of Ultra Chenille. With about 1/2 inch extending past the end of the hook, mount the chenille to the top of the hook shank with four tight thread wraps.

Step 3. Fold the chenille out of the way; using close, tight wraps, move the thread to the front of the hook shank.

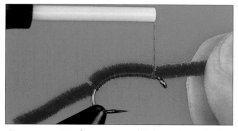

Step 4. With your right hand, pull the chenille over the top of the hook shank. While holding it in position, use your left hand to take four tight thread wraps to secure the chenille.

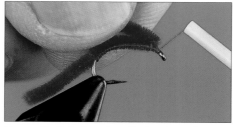

Step 5. Pull the chenille back and using close, tight wraps, move the thread forward to just behind the hook eye. Tie off the thread and cut the excess.

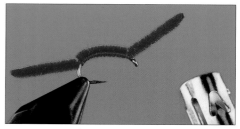

Step 6. With a lighter or match held to one side of the end of the chenille, carefully melt the end into a taper to seal it. Then lacquer the chenille tie-down thread wraps and the head.

Optional:
Weighted San Juan Worm

If more weight is desired, you can add copper wire to the hook shank.

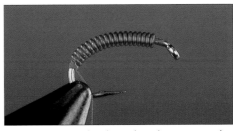

Step 1. Tie in the thread and wrap it to the rear. Take a length of wire and starting at the rear, wrap the wire forward with close, tight wraps. Cut off the excess wire and push the ends tight against the adjoining wraps.

Step 2. Use tight thread wraps to form a taper that butts up against the rearmost wrap of wire. Then mount the chenille at the rear, and wrap the thread forward between the wire wraps.

Beaded San Juan Worm

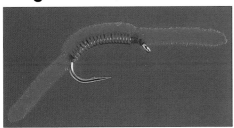

Step 3. At the front of the wire wraps, form a thread taper to hold the wire in position. Pull the chenille forward and secure it with four tight thread wraps. Tie off the thread, lacquer the thread wraps, and taper the chenille ends.

Step 1. Tie a tight overhand knot in the middle of a 2-inch length of chenille. Slide the bead, wide opening first, onto the chenille; then slide the bead onto the hook with the knot to the rear. Mount the hook in the vise.

Step 2. Pinch the bead with your left fingers and pull the knot into the wide end of the bead. Then slide the bead to the back of the hook shank. Tie in the thread behind the hook eye, and form a tapered head as shown.

Step 3. Push the bead against the thread wraps with the chenille on top of the hook shank. Take four tight thread wraps over the chenille in front of the bead; then fold back the chenille and wrap the thread forward. Tie off and cut the thread.

Step 4. Fold the rear chenille forward and tie in the thread behind the bead. Take 5 thread wraps to the rear; then wrap the thread forward to the tie-in position.

Step 5. Pinch the rear chenille to the top of the hook shank, and take four tight, close wraps over the chenille close to the bead.

Step 6. Tie off the thread by placing 3 half-hitches over the thread wraps. Cut the chenille to the desired length; then use a lighter or match and melt each chenille end to a taper. Lacquer the front and rear thread wraps.

Lashed and Extended Bodies—Chenille

Palomino Midge

Originator: Brett Smith
Hook: Scud, 2X wide, 2X short, 2X heavy, sizes 18-22
Thread: Black 8/0, or color to match abdomen
Abdomen: New Dub or Magic Dub, black, brown, olive, gray, or red
Wing case: White Z-lon or Antron yarn
Thorax: Black dubbing or color to match abdomen
Antennae/gills: Butts ends of wing case

Palomino Caddis Pupa

Originator: Brett Smith
Hook: Scud, 2X wide, 2X short, 2X heavy, sizes 14-16
Thread: Olive 6/0, or color to match abdomen
Abdomen: Ultra Chenille or Micro Chenille, olive or tan
Thorax: Olive or tan dubbing color to match abdomen
Wing: Fine long-fiber Antron dubbing, light olive or yellow for tan abdomen.
Optional wing: Emergent, Deer hair mixed with dubbing, color to match abdomen.
Legs: Brown partridge feather fibers
Head: Green or tan dubbing color to match abdomen

Note: These midge and caddis pupa imitations are easy to tie and are effective in both streams and lakes.

Palomino Midge, Black

Step 1. Mount the hook in the vise. Tie in the thread at the front of the hook. Using close tight thread wraps, move the thread back to the position shown.

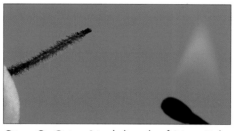

Step 2. Cut a 1-inch length of New Dub. With a match or lighter, hold one end of the chenille off to the side of the flame and melt the end to a taper.

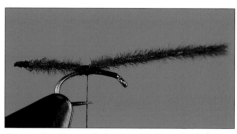

Step 3. Extend the melted end of New Dub one shank-length behind the tie-in position, and mount it on top of the hook shank as shown. Then clip the butt end and wrap the thread back to the rear.

Step 4. Cut a 1-inch length of white Z-lon or Antron yarn. Mount the yarn on top of the hook shank at the tie-in position; then clip the excess yarn. With tight thread wraps, cover end of the yarn, and wrap the thread back to the rear tie-in position.

Step 5. Use a dubbing that matches the color of the abdomen, and dub the body as shown, stopping three or four thread wraps behind the hook eye.

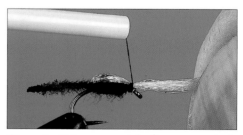

Step 6. Using your right fingers to pinch the end of the yarn, fold it forward over the top of the dubbed thorax. Hold the yarn snug. Take the bobbin in your left hand and secure the yarn with 4 tight wraps.

Palomino Caddis Pupa

Step 7. Put a small amount of dubbing on the thread and dub over the thread wraps. Then fold back the butt ends of the yarn and wrap the thread forward to the hook eye. Tie off the thread and finish the head.

Step 8. Cut the butt ends of the yarn to a length about equal to the length of the wing case.

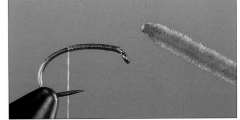

Step 1. Mount a hook in the vise. Tie in the thread at the front of the hook shank and wrap to the rear as shown. Cut 1-inch length of chenille, and use a lighter to melt one end into a taper.

Step 2. Position the tapered end one shank-length behind the rearmost thread wrap. Mount the chenille on top of the hook shank and secure with four tight thread wraps.

Step 3. Trim the butt end of the chenille. Move the thread back to the rear tie-in position. Place some dubbing on the thread and wrap forward to the position shown.

Step 4. Form a **dubbing loop** (p. 38) about 2 inches long. Place a small amount of the long-strand dubbing into the loop and spin it tight to form a dubbing brush.

Step 5. Take 3-5 wraps of the dubbing brush; then tie-off the brush and cut off the excess. Use a **dubbing teaser** (p. 30) to tease out the long fibers and brush them to the rear.

Step 6. Strip 8-10 fibers from a partridge feather. Using the **bundled-fiber throat legs** method (p. 38), mount the fibers to the bottom of the hook shank.

Step 7. Add some dubbing to the thread, and dub the head; then tie off and finish the head.

Optional: Palomino Emergent Caddis

Step 1. Form the abdomen as above in Steps 1-4.

Step 2. Clean and stack (p. 22) a small bunch of deer hair and mix in a small amount long-fibered Antron dubbing. Use the **bundled-fiber downwing** method (p. 44) to mount the wing to the hook as shown. Then dub the head, and tie off and finish the head.

Lashed and Extended Bodies—Furled Yarn

Furled Midge Pupa

Hook: Scud, 2X wide, 2X short, 2X heavy, sizes 18-22
Thread: Black 8/0, or color to match abdomen
Abdomen: Black (or color to match natural) Antron yarn, furled
Gills: White Antron yarn
Thorax: Fine black dubbing, or color to match abdomen

Furled Damsel Nymph

Hook: Nymph, 2XH, 1XL, sizes 14-16
Thread: Olive 6/0
Abdomen: Olive Antron yarn, furled
Wing case: Olive Antron yarn
Thorax: Olive dubbing
Legs: Butt ends of wing case
Eyes: Small glass-bead eyes or mono eyes

Note: Furled bodies are excellent for extended bodies. Many materials that are thin or stranded can be shaped into extended bodies with this technique. Add strands of Krystal Flash or any other flashy or colored material to the yarn before it is furled for more variety.

Furled Midge Pupa

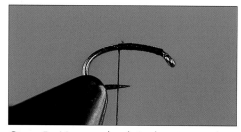

Step 1. Mount a hook in the vise, and tie in the thread at the front of the hook shank. With tight close wraps move the thread back to the position shown.

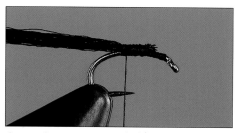

Step 2. Cut a 2-inch length of Antron yarn. Mount one end of the yarn to the top of the hook shank; cover the yarn butt ends and move the thread to the rear.

Step 3. Pinch the end of the yarn with your right thumb and forefinger; then twist the yarn clockwise into a tight cord. The tightness of twists will determine the tightness of the body.

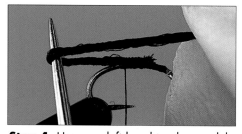

Step 4. Use your left hand to place a dubbing needle at the position where you want the body extension to end (about the length of the hook shank), and then fold the twisted yarn over the needle as shown.

Step 5. Remove the dubbing needle from the yarn while still pinching the yarn with your right fingers. Then move your right fingers, with the pinched yarn, back to the tie-off position and secure it with 3 thread wraps; trim the excess.

Step 6. Cut a 1-inch length of white Antron yarn and mount it on top of the hook shank at the tie-in position. Wrap the thread forward, stopping 3 to 4 thread wraps back from the hook eye as shown.

Step 7. Trim the yarn at the rear close to the thread wraps. Wrap the thread back to the rear tie-in position, covering the butt ends of the yarn.

Step 8. Using a small amount of fine dubbing on the thread, dub the thorax as shown.

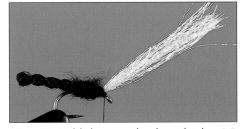

Step 9. Fold the yarn back and take 4-5 thread wraps in front of the yarn to push it away from the hook eye; then tie off and finish the head. Trim the yarn to the desired length.

Furled Damsel Nymph

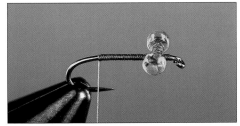

Step 1. Mount a hook and tie in the thread at the front of the hook shank. Mount the **eyes** (p. 50); then using tight, close wraps move the thread to the rear position as shown.

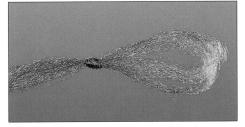

Step 2. Cut two 8-inch lengths of Antron yarn. Place them together and fold them in half. Tie an overhand knot at the folded end as shown.

Step 3. Position the knot at the desired body length, and mount two of the yarn stands on top of the hook shank at the tie-in position as shown.

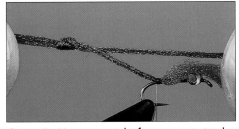

Step 4. Use your right fingers to twist the yarn tight. Then pinch the yarn loop with your left fingers and pull the yarn to the rear as shown. Release your left fingers from the loop and let the yarn furl. Secure the furled yarn at the tie-in position.

Step 5. Cut the yarn loop to the desired length to imitate the damselfly's gill/paddles. Dub over the body tie-down wraps. Fold back the yarn and dub the thorax and around the eyes as shown.

Step 6. Fold the tag ends of the yarn forward and secure with 3 tight thread wraps behind the hook eye. Then fold the tag end down and to the rear and secure in position by wrapping back toward the eyes as shown.

Step 7. Wrap the thread forward forming the head; then tie off and finish the head. Cut the yarn legs to length.

Step 8. Trim the yarn, close to the thread wraps, so that 10 or 12 strands per side remain to imitate the legs.

Chapter 3

Strand Bodies

Wrapped single- or multi-strand materials are excellent for forming nymph bodies. The variety of stranded materials used in fly tying seems endless and the number grows as new materials continue to appear. This simple body-forming technique is fast and easy.

Strand Bodies—Wire

Brassie

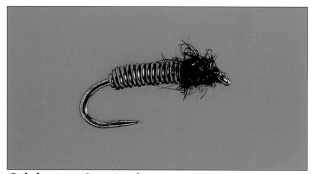

Originator: Gene Lynch
Hook: Nymph, 2X long, 2X heavy, sizes 12-20
Thread: Black or color to match head dubbing, 6/0 or 8/0
Body: Brass, copper or colored wire; the diameter of the wire should be smaller than the hook wire diameter
Head: Black or dark brown dubbing

Metallic Caddis Larva

Hook: Scud, 2X heavy, sizes 12-18
Thread: Olive 6/0 or 8/0
Abdomen: Copper or green wire; the diameter of the wire should be smaller than the hook wire diameter
Legs: Natural gray CDC fibers
Wing buds: Option for pupa, two gray CDC feather tips
Thorax: Peacock herl; option for pupa, Arizona Synthetic Peacock Dubbing
Head: Brass bead, size to match hook size

Note: The Brassie and similar wire-wrapped flies are good imitations of midge or caddis larvae and pupae that sink like rocks.

Brassie

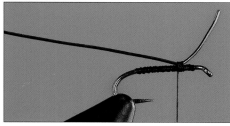

Step 1. Mount a hook in the vise. Tie in the thread behind the hook eye and wrap it to the rear then back to the front tie-in position. Cut length of wire and mount it on top of the hook shank with four tight wraps.

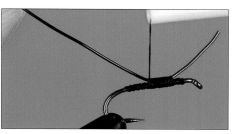

Step 2. Use the **shank wrap** method (p. 18) to secure the wire to the top of the hook shank, stopping at the rear thread wraps.

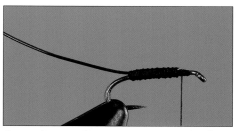

Step 3. Cut the excess wire at the front close to the hook shank. Then wrap the thread forward and cover the tag end.

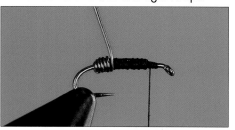

Step 4. Take the first wire wrap behind the rear thread wraps; then wrap the wire forward with close tight wraps.

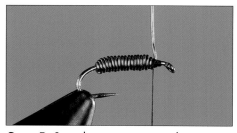

Step 5. Stop the wire wraps at the position shown, and take three tight thread wraps to secure the wire. Cut the excess wire close to the hook shank and bind down the tag end.

Step 6. Dub the head; then tie off the thread and finish the head.

Metallic Caddis Larva

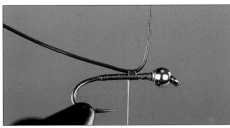

Step 1. Slide a brass bead onto the hook, and mount the hook in the vise. Tie in the thread and secure the brass bead behind the hook eye to form the **bead head** (p. 51). Mount the wire at the position shown.

Step 2. Form a wire body as shown in the previous Brassie Steps 2-4. Mount the peacock herls in front of the wire as shown, and cut the excess close to the hook shank.

Step 3. Wrap the herls forward and secure with 3 thread wraps behind the brass bead.

Step 4. Use the **bundled-fiber throat legs** method (p. 38) to mount 8-12 CDC feather fibers to the bottom of the hook shank.

Step 6. Trim the butt ends of the CDC fibers. Place a small amount of Peacock Dubbing on the thread and dub over the exposed thread wraps as shown. Then tie off the thread close to the brass bead and lacquer the thread wraps.

Optional: Metallic Caddis Pupa

Step 1. Place a hook in the vise and secure a brass bead. Form a body as shown in Metallic Caddis Larva Steps 1-2. Use the **bundled-fiber throat legs** method (p. 38) to secure 8-10 CDC fibers on the bottom of the hook shank, Trim the butt ends.

Step 2. Strip the bottom fibers off two CDC feathers. Use the **slide mount** (p. 18) method to secure one feather tip to each side of the hook shank as shown.

Step 3. Trim away the butt end of the feathers close to the thread wraps. Dub over the thread wraps. Tie off the thread close to the brass bead and lacquer the wraps.

Strand Bodies—Plastic Tubing

Larva Lace Midge

Hook: Nymph 2X long, 2X heavy, sizes 14-20
Thread: Red 8/0 or color to match body
Body: Red, olive, brown or black Larva Lace or similar
tubing, size to match hook size
Head: Red dubbing or color to match body

Larva Lace Caddis Larva

Hook: Scud/shrimp, sizes 12-18
Thread: Brown 8/0 for the head, green 8/0 for the body
Rib: Option for pupae, fine tan or white Antron dubbing
brush, to imitate gills
Abdomen: Olive, brown or tan Larva Lace or similar
tubing, size to match hook
Thorax: Olive dubbing
Wing buds: Option for pupa, dark brown or black
Anton yarn
Legs: Brown mottled hen hackle fibers or brown CDC
feather fibers
Head: Optional, brown glass or brass bead

Note: Larva Lace and other plastic tubings are ideal for forming lightweight segmented bodies. These tubings come in different diameters, but they can also be stretched to reduce their size. The interior of the tubing can be filled with mineral oil, wire, tinsel, or floss for added attraction.

Larva Lace Midge

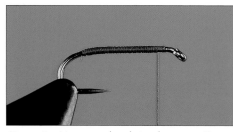

Step 1. Mount a hook in the vise. Tie in the thread and wrap the thread back to the rear of the hook then forward again to the position shown.

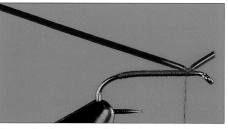

Step 2. Cut a length of tubing and mount one end of tubing with four tight thread wraps to the top of the hook shank as shown.

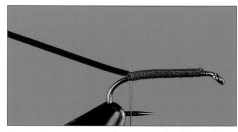

Step 3. Trim away the tag end of the tubing. Use the **shank wrap** method (p. 18) to secure the tubing to the top of the hook shank with close, tight wraps to the position shown. Then wrap the thread to the front tie-in position.

Larva Lace Caddis Larva

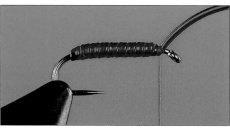

Step 4. Stretch the tubing to form a smaller first wrap behind the thread wraps. Then relax the tension and with close, tight wraps, move the tubing to the forward position. Secure the tubing with 4 tight thread wraps, and cut the excess.

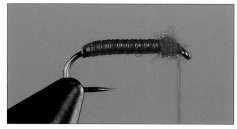

Step 5. Dub the head, then tie off and finish the head.

Step 1. Slide a glass bead onto the hook and mount the hook in the vise. Secure the **glass bead head** (p. 51) behind the hook eye. Use brown thread in front of the bead and olive thread behind the bead.

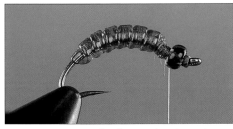

Step 2. Form a body as shown in Larva Lace Midge Steps 1-4, stopping at the position shown.

Step 3. Dub the thorax, stopping just short of the bead.

Step 4. Use the **bundled-fiber throat legs** method (p. 38) to mount 6-8 hen hackle fibers to the bottom of the hook shank.

Step 5. Trim away the fiber butts close to the hook shank. Apply a small amount of dubbing to the thread and dub over the thread wraps. Tie off the thread directly behind the bead. Cut the thread and lacquer the wraps.

Option: Larva Lace Pupa

With a few small alterations, the Larva Lace Larva pattern can be changed into a very good deep-water caddis pupa pattern.

Step 1. Slide a brass bead onto the hook, and mount the hook in the vise. Tie in the thread, and secure the **brass bead** (p. 51) behind the hook eye. Tie in the tubing with the **shank wrap** method (p. 18), and leave the thread at the rear tie-in position as shown.

Step 2. Mount the tan Antron **wire core dubbing brush** (p. 33) at the rear tie-in position. Wrap the thread forward to the position shown, covering the butt ends of the dubbing brush and tubing.

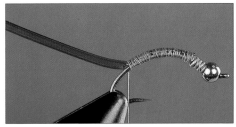

Step 3. Wrap the tubing forward, leaving a small gap between each wrap—just enough space to allow the dubbing bush wire to slip between the wraps. Secure the tubing at the position shown and cut the excess.

Step 4. Wrap the dubbing brush forward, placing the wire in the gaps between the tubing wraps. With each wrap, preen the fibers to the rear as shown. Secure the dubbing brush at the front of the tubing. Cut the excess and trim the fibers to shape.

Step 5. Use a small amount of dubbing to dub the rear half of the thorax. Mount a short length of Anton yarn, and form the **cut Antron wing buds** (p. 44).

Step 6. Take 8-10 CDC feather fibers and use the **bundled-fiber throat legs** method (p. 38) to mount them on the underside of the hook shank as shown.

Step 7. Dub the front of the thorax. Then tie off the thread behind the brass bead. Cut the thread and lacquer the thread wraps.

Strand Bodies—Latex

Latex Larva

Hook: Nymph 2X long, 2X heavy, sizes 14-20
Thread: Olive 8/0
Underbody: Olive (or color to match natural) thread
Body: Latex, 1/8-inch strip (optional: color with waterproof marker)
Optional wings: Pupa, duck quill sections coated with Flexament
Thorax: Brown-rabbit/Antron-dubbing mix
Head: Optional for larva or pupa, glass or brass bead

Latex Mayfly Nymph

Hook: Nymph, 2X long, 2X heavy, sizes 14-20
Thread: Brown 8/0
Tail: Brown mottled hen hackle fibers
Underbody: Brown thread
Abdomen: 1/8-inch wide tan latex strip or Scud Back
Wing case: Latex strip from abdomen
Thorax: Brown dubbing, picked out

Note: Wrapped latex strips form realistic bodies that are easy to color with waterproof markers or with a colored thread underbody that will show through the latex. When cutting a strip from a latex sheet on a cutting board, place a sheet of paper over the latex, then use a razor guided by a straightedge to cut through the paper and latex at the same time.

Latex Larva

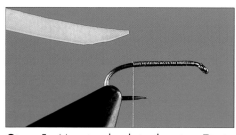

Step 1. Mount a hook in the vise. Tie in the thread behind the hook eye and move the thread to the rear. Cut a 1/8-inch strip from a latex sheet and taper one end as shown.

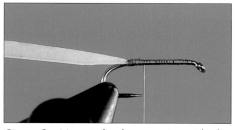

Step 2. Mount the latex strip with the straight edge facing up, as shown. Then wrap the thread forward, forming a smooth underbody.

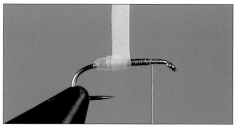

Step 3. With the thread positioned at the front, wrap the latex strip forward with slightly overlapping wraps to form a segmented body as shown. Continue wrapping to the front tie-off position.

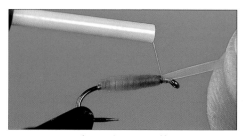

Step 4. When the tie-off position is reached, take two tight wraps over the latex. Then stretch the latex as shown and take three more wraps over the latex. While still stretching the latex, cut it close to the hook shank.

Step 5. Dub the thorax; then tie off and finish the head.

Latex Caddis Pupa

If you tie this pattern using natural cream latex, carry a few colors of waterproof marker while fishing, and match the color of any natural with a few quick pen strokes.

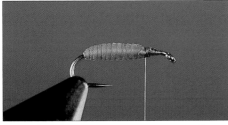

Step 1. Form a latex body as shown above in Steps 1-4

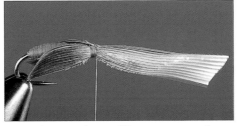

Step 2. Use the **quill emerger wings** method (p. 44) to mount a quill section to each side of the hook shank

Step 3. Dub the thorax; then tie off the thread and finish the head.

Latex Mayfly Nymph

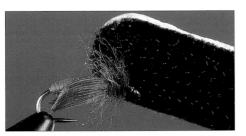

Step 4. Use a dubbing teaser to pick-out the dubbing fibers as shown.

Step 1. Mount a hook in the vise. Tie in the thread at the front and wrap it to the rear. Mount 4-6 hen hackle fibers on top of the hook shank as shown.

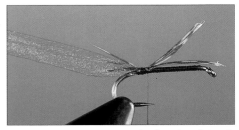

Step 2. Taper one end of a Scud Back strip. At the rear tie-in position, mount the latex strip with the straight edge facing up.

Step 3. Wrap the thread in layers to form a tapered body and bind down the tail fibers. Then cut the excess fibers close to the hook shank.

Step 4. Wrap the latex strip forward with overlapping wraps, and secure with 3 thread wraps at the position shown.

Step 5. Fold the latex strip back and wrap the thread back over the base of the folded strip, binding it onto the top of the last abdomen segment as shown.

Step 6. Dub over the thorax section, stopping 3-4 thread wraps behind the hook eye.

Step 7. To form the wing case, pull the latex strip forward over the top of the thorax with your right fingers. Then with the bobbin in your left hand, take four wraps over the latex as shown. Clip the excess latex and tie off the thread and finish the head.

Step 8. Use a bobbin or dubbing teaser to pick-out the dubbing on the bottom of the thorax to form the legs.

Strand Bodies—Floss

Partridge and Green Soft Hackle

Hook: Nymph, 2X heavy, size10-16
Thread: Green 8/0
Abdomen: Green floss
Thorax: Tan hare's ear dubbing
Hackle: Gray partridge

Bead Thorax Partridge and Red

Hook: Nymph, 2X heavy, size12-16
Thread: Red 8/0
Rib: Fine silver Mylar tinsel
Abdomen: Red floss
Thorax: Spirit River two-diameter counterdrilled brass
bead, size to match hook
Hackle: Gray partridge

Note: Soft-hackle style flies are one of fly-fishing's earliest patterns, and they are simple and effective. Floss, used often for these flies, forms a slim, attractive body. Synthetic floss is easier to use than silk floss, but many tiers still prefer silk.

Partridge and Green Soft Hackle

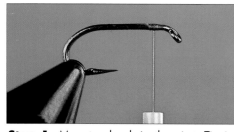

Step 1. Mount a hook in the vise. Tie in the thread 3-4 wraps behind the hook eye and wrap it rearward with 4-6 tight, close wraps. Then wrap forward 3 wraps.

Step 2. Use the **preparing hackle feathers** (p. 45) method to prepare the feather as shown.

Step 3. Mount the feather, with the concave side facing up, on top of the hook shank with 4 tight wraps as shown. Clip the excess stem close to the thread wraps.

Step 4. Place the floss in a bobbin and wax the first 1/2 inch of floss to keep it from slipping. Use three tight thread wraps to mount the floss directly behind the butt end of the feather as shown.

Step 5. Trim the excess floss. Wrap the floss rearward in close, tight wraps. Keep the floss flat so that it looks like a smooth ribbon. If the floss starts to twist into a cord, spin the bobbin counterclockwise to remove the twist.

Step 6. With close, tight wraps, move the floss forward to the tie-in position. If the floss ribbon starts to split, unwrap it one turn and twist it close to the hook shank to rejoin the ribbon. Tie-off and trim the excess floss.

Step 7. Place a small amount of dubbing on the thread, and dub over the thorax area, covering the thread wraps. Then wrap the thread to the front of the feather.

Step 8. Grasp the feather stem with hackle pliers held in your right fingers and raise the feather vertically. With your left fingers, fold the fibers back as shown. Gently preen the barbs back a few times, until they hold their position.

Step 9. Take 1 or 2 wraps with the hackle as shown. These are sparse flies, and one hackle wrap is often enough.

Bead Thorax Partridge and Red

Step 10. Use three tight thread wraps to secure the hackle. Trim the excess feather as shown. Tie off the thread and finish the head.

Step 1. Slide a brass bead onto the hook shank with the small end toward the hook eye. Mount the hook in the vise. Tie in the thread behind the bead.

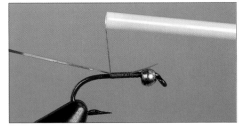

Step 2. Mount a length of Mylar tinsel on top of the hook shank at the tie-in position with the silver side down. Use the **shank wrap** method (p. 18) to keep the tinsel on top of the hook shank as you wrap the thread to the rear, as shown.

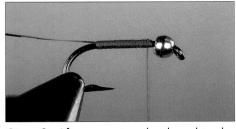

Step 3. After wrapping the thread to the rear, return the thread forward to the tie-in position with close tight wraps, forming a smooth underbody.

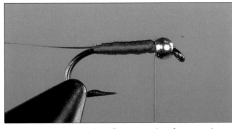

Step 4. Mount the floss at the forward tie-in position and form a smooth body as shown previously in Steps 3-6. Secure the floss close to the back of the bead and trim the excess.

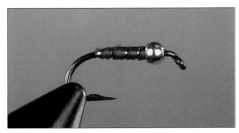

Step 5. Wrap the tinsel ribbing forward; secure it behind the bead and trim the excess. Tie off and cut the thread. Place a drop of head cement on the thread wraps. Push the bead to the rear so it's snug against the body, covering the thread wraps.

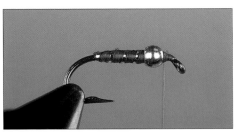

Step 6. Tie in the thread in front of the bead, and build a small taper to hold the bead in position.

Step 7. Prepare the feather (p. 21) and mount it by the tip to the hook shank. Clip the excess as shown.

Step 8. Preen the barbs back and take 1-2 hackle wraps; then secure and clip the excess feather as shown. Tie off and finish the head.

Strand Bodies—Chenille

Woolly Worm-Black

Hook: Nymph, 2X-4X long, 2X heavy, sizes 2-12
Thread: Black or color to match body
Tail: Red wool or poly yarn, trimmed short
Underbody: Optional, lead wire
Body: Black, green, or brown chenille, or color of choice
Hackle: Grizzly, brown, or color of choice saddle feather
Head: Spirit River two-diameter counterdrilled brass bead, size to match hook size

Woolly Bugger-Olive

Hook: Nymph, 3X-4X long, sizes 2-14
Thread: Olive or color to match body
Tail: Olive marabou, (optional: Krystal Flash strands, color of choice, mixed with marabou)
Underbody: Optional, lead wire
Rib: Optional, gold or silver wire
Body: Olive, black, or brown chenille, or color of your choice (option: Crystal Chenille)
Hackle: Olive grizzly saddle feather, or color to match body or of choice
Legs: Optional, rubber legs
Eyes: Optional, lead dumbbell
Head: Optional, Spirit River two-diameter counterdrilled brass bead

Note: This style of fly probably catches more fish than any other. It is easy to tie and has many variations.

Black Woolly Worm

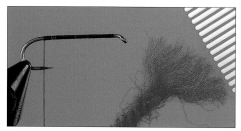

Step 1. Mount a hook in the vise. Tie in the thread at the front of the hook and advance the thread to the rear. Comb out one end of the yarn as shown.

Step 2. Mount the brushed end of the yarn at rear of the hook shank; then secure the yarn to the top of the hook shank stopping about 1/4 inch behind the front tie-in position. Cut the excess yarn and return the thread to the rear tie-in position.

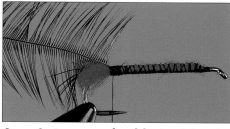

Step 3. Prepare a **hackle** (p. 47) to be tip-mounted, and mount it by the tip at the rear tie-in position with the glossy side facing you.

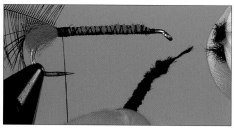

Step 4. Use your fingernails to strip off the chenille fibers and expose about 1/4 inch of thread as shown. Mount the chenille's exposed thread at the rear tie-in position. Wrap the thread to the front tie-in position.

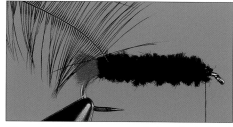

Step 5. Take one wrap of chenille behind the feather, then with tight, close turns, wrap the chenille forward and secure it 1/4 inch behind the eye. Trim the excess. For a neater body, preen the chenille fibers back with each wrap.

Step 6. Palmer (p. 48) the hackle forward, preening the fibers back with each wrap; then secure the feather in front of the body as shown. Trim the excess and finish the head.

Optional:
Bead Head Woolly Worm

Woolly Bugger, Olive

Step 1. Mount a hook in the vise. Tie in the thread behind the hook eye and wrap it to the rear tie-in position. Strip the marabou barbs from 1 or 2 feathers, keeping the tips even.

Step 4. Counter-wrap the wire ribbing as shown. Continue wrapping the wire forward to the tie-off position. Secure the wire with three tight thread wraps, and cut off the excess. Tie off and finish the head.

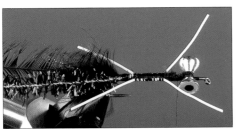

Step 2. Mount the hackle and chenille. Move the thread to the middle of the body. Mount a length of rubber leg material to each side of the hook shank as shown in the **legs** methods (p. 37). Then advance the thread to the front tie-in position.

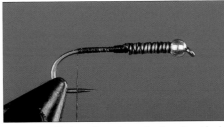

Step 1. Slide a bead on the hook with the small hole facing the hook eye. Mount the hook in the vise. Use the **bead head** method (p. 51) to weight the body and secure the head. Move the thread to the rear tie-in position.

Step 2. Mount the marabou on top of the hook shank so the tail extension is about the length of the hook shank. Wrap the thread forward and trim the excess marabou; cover the butt ends with thread. Then return the thread to the rear tie-in position.

Optional:
Eyed/Legged Woolly Bugger

Step 3. Wrap the chenille forward, stopping behind the eyes. Secure the chenille with three tight wraps, but do not trim the excess. Palmer the hackle forward, secure it behind the eyes, and clip the excess. Wrap the thread to the front of the eyes.

Step 2. Mount the tail, hackle, and chenille. Complete the body as shown in Steps 1-6. Cover the thread wraps behind the bead with a small amount of dubbing that matches the color of the body. Tie off the thread behind the bead and lacquer the wraps.

Step 3. Mount the feather, chenille and a length of gold wire for the rib. Wrap the body and hackle as shown in the previous Steps 2-6.

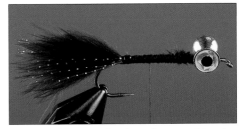

Step 1. Mount a hook in the vise. Use the **mounting eyes** method (p. 50) to secure the eyes a distance of 8-12 thread wraps behind the hook eye. Mount the marabou tail, and on each side of the tail mount 2-6 strands of Krystal Flash.

Step 4. Take one wrap of chenille behind the eyes to cover the thread wraps; then make a figure-eight wrap around the eyes, and finish with one wrap in front of the eyes. Secure the chenille and trim the excess. Tie off the thread and finish the head.

Strand Bodies—Twisted Yarn

Serendipity

Hook: Scud or nymph, 2X heavy, sizes 12-20
Thread: Olive or color to match natural
Rib: Optional, fine silver, gold, or copper wire
Body: Olive Antron yarn or Z-lon (or color of natural), adjust the thickness of the strand to match the hook size
Head: Deer or caribou hair, spun and trimmed to shape

Yarn Caddis Larva

Hook: Scud or nymph, 2X heavy, sizes 12-18
Weight: Optional, wrapped under thorax area only
Thread: Brown or color to match natural
Rib: Optional, fine wire or Krystal Flash
Abdomen: Green Antron yarn or Z-lon (or color to match natural), adjust the thickness of the strand to match the hook size
Thorax: Brown dubbing
Legs: Brown mottled hen hackle fibers
Optional pupa hackle: Light dun CDC
Head: Optional, brass bead head

Note: Twisted-yarn bodies are durable, segmented, and easily tied. This body style can be used on patterns of all sizes. The Serendipity is one of the better smaller flies. It is used to imitate midge pupae in streams and lakes. The caddis larva pattern is easily changed to an effective caddis pupa pattern.

Serendipity

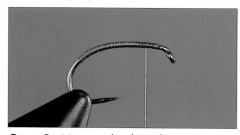

Step 1. Mount a hook in the vise. Tie in the thread at the front of the hook shank; wrap the thread to the rear and back to the front, laying a thread base as shown.

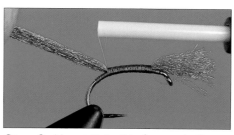

Step 2. Mount 2- to 3-inch strand of yarn at the front of the hook shank. Use the **shank wrap** method (p. 18) to keep the yarn on top of the hook shank, and wrap the thread to the rear. Return the thread to the forward tie-in position; trim the front excess yarn.

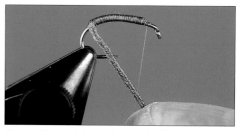

Step 3. Holding the end of the yarn in your fingers, form a cord by twisting the strand in the clockwise direction. A clockwise twist will keep the strand in a tight cord as it is wrapped.

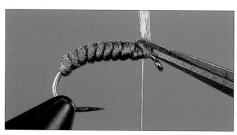

Step 4. Use tight, close wraps to advance to cord to the front tie-in position. Twist the yarn strand as needed to keep it in a tight cord. Secure the yarn with 4 tight thread wraps and trim the excess yarn.

Step 5. Use the **hair cleaning and stacking** method (p. 22) to prepare a small clump of deer hair. Trim the tips and butts evenly.

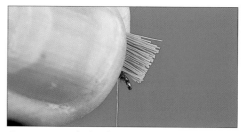

Step 6. With the butt ends of the hair facing forward, pinch the bunch of hair with your left thumb and forefinger; then position the hair over the hook shank as shown.

Step 7. Use the **pinch wrap** method (p. 18) to mount the hair to the top of the hook shank. Place 3-4 tight thread wraps, on top of one another, directly at the tie-in position. This will cause the hair to flare out.

Step 8. Use your left fingers to preen back the deer hair from the hook eye, then wrap the thread forward. Tie off and cut the thread.

Step 9. Trim the deer hair to shape by rounding the head and cutting the wing at an angle. Put a drop of head cement on the thread wraps.

Optional, Ribbed Serendipity

When a rib is desired to accent the body segments, tie in the wire with the yarn. Then after the body is formed, wrap the wire forward, placing it between the body wraps.

Yarn Caddis Larva

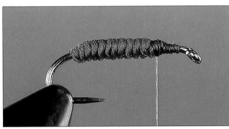

Step 1. Mount a hook in the vise and form the abdomen as shown in Steps 1-4 of the previous sequence.

Step 2. Dub over the thorax, stopping 4-5 wraps behind the hook eye.

Step 3. Use the **bundled-fiber throat legs** method (p. 38) to mount the feather fibers below the hook shank, and trim the excess. Place a small amount of dubbing on the thread, and dub over the thread wraps. Then tie off and finish the head.

Bead Head Yarn Caddis Pupa

Step 1. Slide a bead on the hook. Mount the hook in the vise. Use the **bead head** method (p. 51) to secure the bead and weight the thorax. Form the abdomen as shown above, using 2-4 strands of twisted orange or copper Krystal Flash for ribbing.

Step 2. Dub the thorax with tan Hare-Tron dubbing, and brush out with a dubbing teaser. Then mount the legs as shown in Step 3 of the previous sequence.

Step 3. Mount a light dun CDC feather by its tip, and take 1-3 wraps behind the bead. Secure the feather with 3 thread wraps and trim the excess.

Step 4. Place a small amount brown dubbing on the thread. Preen back the CDC fibers and dub over the thread wraps behind the bead. Tie off and cut the thread; then cement the thread wraps.

Strand Bodies—Twisted Yarn

Brooks Stone

Originator: Charles Brooks
Hook: Nymph, 2X heavy, 3X-4X long, sizes 4-8
Underbody: Lead wire
Thread: Black 6/0
Tail: Two black goose biots
Rib: Copper wire
Abdomen: Black yarn
Gills: Two white ostrich herls
Hackle: Brown and grizzly

Box Canyon Stone

Originator: Mims Barker
Hook: Nymph, 2X heavy, 3X-4X long, sizes 2-10
Weight: Lead wire
Thread: Black 6/0
Tail: Two dark brown goose biots
Abdomen: Black yarn, twisted
Wing case: Brown mottled turkey feather section
Thorax: Black dubbing
Legs: Furnace hackle

Note: These heavily weighted patterns, meant to tumble along the stream bottom, are good imitations of the giant stonefly nymphs that occur in Western streams.

Brooks Stone

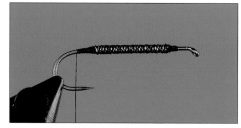

Step 1. Mount a hook in the vise. Use the **direct wrap underbody** method (p. 24) to form the lead wire underbody as shown. Stop the wraps about 1/4 inch behind the hook eye. Advance the thread to the rear.

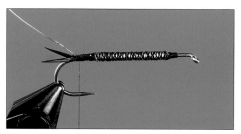

Step 2. At the rear tie-in position, use the **split biot tail** method (p. 25) to mount a goose biot on each side of the hook shank. Take 2-3 thread wraps forward from the tie-in position, and mount the copper wire to the top of the hook shank.

Step 3. Position the thread about 1/8 inch behind the hook eye. Mount a length of yarn to the top of the hook shank, and use the **shank wrap** method (p. 18) to secure the yarn to the top of the hook shank as shown. Trim the front tag of yarn.

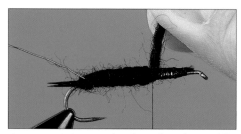

Step 4. Advance the thread to the middle of the shank. Take the first wrap of yarn behind the wire; then wrap the yarn forward forming a smooth body. Stop at the hanging thread and secure the yarn with 4 tight thread wraps.

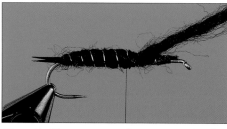

Step 5. Counter-wrap the copper wire forward with evenly spaced wraps to the front of the body. Secure the wire with 4 tight wraps and trim the excess. Move the thread back to the front of the body wraps.

Step 6. Mount 2 ostrich herls. Put the **prepared** (p. 21) hackle feathers together so the stems and barbs match and trim the end stems even. Strip the barbs from the same side of each feather. Mount the feathers together on the hook shank as shown.

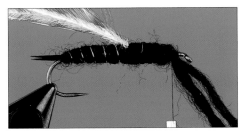

Step 7. Pull the yarn rearward and advance the thread forward. Wrap the yarn to form a thorax of the same diameter as the abdomen. Stop one yarn-wrap back from the hook eye, and secure the yarn with 3 tight thread wraps.

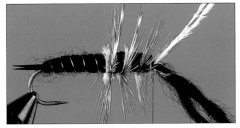

Step 8. Gather the herls and feathers together and take 2-3 wraps forward to the tie-off position. Secure them and trim the excess.

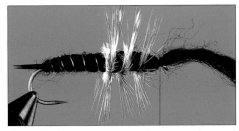

Step 9. Take one wrap of yarn in front of the hackles, secure the yarn, and trim the excess. Tie off the thread and finish the head.

Box Canyon Stone

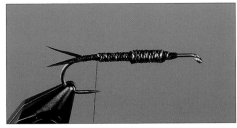

Step 1. Mount a hook in the vise. Use the **double-layer wrap underbody** method (p. 20) to form the lead wire underbody as shown. Move the thread to the rear, and tie in two biots using the **split biot tail** method (p. 25).

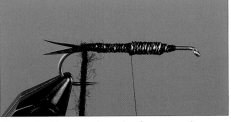

Step 2. Mount a length of yarn at the rear of the hook, and advance the thread to just past mid-shank. Twist the yarn clockwise into a tight cord.

Step 3. Using tight, close wraps, advance the yarn to the tie-off position. Maintain the tight cord by adding clockwise twists as needed. Secure the yarn and trim the excess.

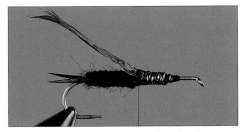

Step 4. From a mottled turkey feather, cut a section that is a little wider than the thorax; then with the dull side facing up, mount one end of the section to the top of the hook shank as shown.

Step 5. Prepare a feather (p. 21), and with the shiny side facing you, mount the tip of the feather on the hook shank.

Step 6. Dub the thorax area, forming an even transition from the abdomen. Stop about 6-8 thread wraps behind the hook eye.

Step 7. Using 3-5 evenly spaced turns, wrap the hackle to the forward tie-off position. Preen back the barbs with each wrap. Secure the feather and trim the excess.

Step 8. Use your left thumb and forefinger to preen the barbs down. Then with your right fingers, pull the turkey feather section forward as shown.

Step 9. Release your left fingers from the barbs, while maintaining pressure on the wing case with your right fingers. With the bobbin in your left hand, take 3 tight wraps over the feather section. Trim the excess, tie-off the thread, and finish the head.

Strand Bodies—Fur Strip

Bead Head Rabbit Leech

Hook: Nymph, 2X heavy, 2X-3X long, sizes 4-10
Thread: Black 6/0 or color to match body
Tail: Brown, black, olive (or color of choice) longitudinally-cut rabbit strip
Tail option: Krystal Flash 2-6 strands per side, color of choice
Body: Rabbit strip end from tail
Body option: Cross-cut rabbit strip
Head: Spirit River two-diameter counterdrilled brass or colored bead, size to match hook
Optional creeper eyes: Dumbbell eyes, size to match hook shank

Bead Head Squirrel Leech

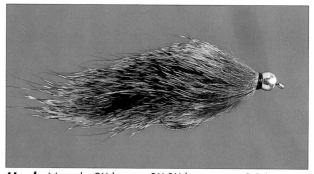

Hook: Nymph, 2X heavy, 2X-3X long, sizes 8-14
Thread: Brown
Optional creeper legs: White or brown, round rubber legs
Tail: Red squirrel, longitudinally-cut strip
Body: Red squirrel strip
Head: Spirit River two-diameter counterdrilled brass bead, size to match hook size
Optional creeper eyes: Dumbbell lead eyes

Note: Wrapped hide-strip bodies are easy to tie, lively in the water, and very durable. You can cut your own strips or buy them pre-cut. A cross-cut strip produces a slimmer profile, while a longitudinally cut strip causes the hair to flare out, producing a wider body that pulsates when stripped through the water.

Bead Head Rabbit Leech

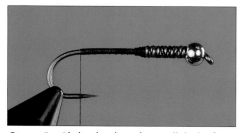

Step 1. Slide the bead, small hole first, onto the hook. Mount the hook in the vise. Then using the **bead head** method (p. 51), secure the bead and form the underbody as shown. Advance the thread to the rear tie-in position.

Step 2. Take a precut rabbit strip and, on the end where the hair extends back past the hide, trim the hide to a point as shown.

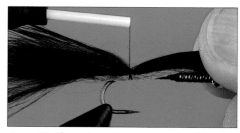

Step 3. Place the strip atop the shank so that the pointed end extends one shank length rearward of the tie-in position. Divide the hairs over the tie-in position, and take 4 tight thread wraps on the hide only, as shown.

Optional: Eyed Rabbit Creeper

Step 4. Advance the thread forward. Take the butt end of the strip and use close, tight turns to wrap the strip forward to the back of the bead. With each wrap preen the hairs back as shown.

Step 5. Divide the hair over the front tie-off position, and take 4 tight thread wraps over the hide to secure the strip. Then cut the excess strip, tie off the thread, and cement the thread wraps.

When the eye is mounted on the top of the hook shank it flips the fly over in the water so the hook point rides up, making it less likely on the snag to bottom.

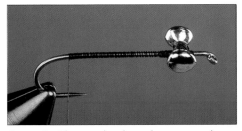

Step 1. Place a hook in the vise and use the **eye mounting** method (p. 50) to secure a pair of eyes about a 1/4 inch behind the hook eye as shown. Then wrap the thread to the rear tie-in position.

Step 2. Prepare the tail as shown in Step 2 of the previous sequence. Mount it at the tie-in position with the hide side facing upward. Use 4 tight wraps and trim the excess fur strip. Mount 2-6 Krystal Flash strands to each side of the tail.

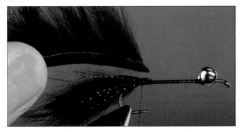

Step 3. Take a cross-cut strip and trim to a point the end opposite the natural slant of the hair as shown. Then mount the trimmed end of the strip at the rear tie in position, and advance the thread to the back of the eyes.

Bead Head Squirrel Leech

Step 4. Wrap the strip forward with close, tight wraps, preening the hair back with each wrap. Wrap the strip to the eyes, secure with 4 thread wraps, and trim the excess. Dub the head with a similar color dubbing. Tie off the thread and finish the head.

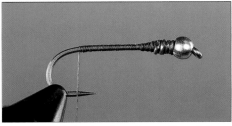

Step 1. Slide the bead, small end first, onto the hook. Mount the hook in the vise. Then use the **bead head** method (p. 51) with lead wire wrapped as shown; secure the wire and bead. Advance the thread to the rear tie-in position.

Step 2. Take a precut squirrel strip and at the end where the hair extends back past the hide, trim the hide to a point as shown.

Step 3. Place the strip atop the shank so that the pointed end extends one shank-length rearward of the tie-in position. Divide the hairs over the tie-in position and take 4 tight thread wraps over the hide only, as shown.

Step 4. Advance the thread forward. Take the butt end of the strip and use close, tight turns to wrap the strip forward to the back of the bead. With each wrap, preen the hairs back as shown.

Step 5. Divide the hair over the front tie-off position and take 4 tight thread wraps over the hide to secure the strip. Then cut the excess strip, tie off the thread, and cement the thread wraps.

Eyed Squirrel Creeper

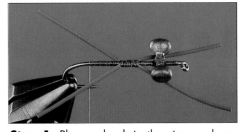

Step 1. Place a hook in the vise, and use the **eye mounting** method (p. 50) to secure a pair of eyes. Advance the thread to the middle of the hook shank, and use the **side-lashed legs** method (p. 37) to mount the legs as shown. Move the thread to the rear.

Step 2. Prepare and mount the tail, hide side up as shown in Steps 2-3 above. Wrap the strip forward around the legs and take 2 wraps in front of the eyes. Fold the strip back between the eyes, preen the fibers back, tie-off and trim the excess.

Strand Bodies—Dubbing Brush

Dubbing Brush Mayfly Nymph

Hook: Nymph, 2X heavy, 2X long, sizes 10-16, weighted
Thread: Brown
Tail: Red squirrel tail fibers
Body: Red squirrel or other fur spun in a wire-core dubbing brush, clipped to shape
Wing case: Epoxy

Dubbing Brush Dragonfly Nymph

Hook: Nymph, 3X long, 2X heavy, sizes 6-10, weight optional
Thread: Brown or olive
Abdomen: Brown or olive rabbit spun in a wire-core dubbing brush, trimmed to shape
Wing case: 2 hen feathers
Thorax: Dubbing to match body
Legs: Brown or olive medium rubber legs
Eyes: Black mono or plastic

Note: Wire-core dubbing brushes are ideal for forming clipped bodies that imitate nymphs, larvae or scuds. Once the brushes are made, it takes little time to wrap and shape the bodies. When the brush is clipped close to the core, the wire shows through, adding a little sparkle to the fly. Thicker bodies have a lifelike movement when retrieved through the water.

Dubbing Brush Mayfly Nymph

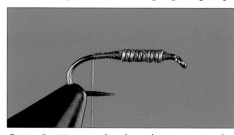

Step 1. Mount a hook in the vise. Use the **underbody lead direct wrap** method (p. 20) to add weight to the hook shank. Advance the thread to the rear.

Step 2. Align the ends of 5-10 squirrel tail fibers and mount them on top of the hook shank. Form a **wire-core dubbing brush** (p. 30) from red squirrel fur. Mount the brush at the rear and trim the excess wire. Advance the thread to the front.

Step 3. Wrap the brush forward with tight, close wraps, preening back each wrap as shown. Continue wrapping to the front tie-off position. Use 4 thread wraps to secure the brush, and trim the excess. Tie off the thread and finish the head.

Step 4. Trim the rear half flat on the bottom. Trim the bottom of the front half even with the hook point. Pick out the underfur to thin out the leg area. Then trim the top of the fly flat.

Step 5. Trim the sides to a taper.

Step 6. Use toothpick to apply a small amount of 5-minute epoxy to the top of the thorax; continue adding epoxy until you have covered the top of the thorax, forming the wing case.

Dubbing Brush Scud

Use olive or tan rabbit fur to form the wire-core dubbing brush for this fly.

Step 1. Form the body as shown above in Steps 2-3.

Step 2. Trim the top, sides, and bottom of the body. Thin out the fibers in the leg area. Leave a few fibers extending rearward for a tail, as shown.

Dubbing Brush Dragonfly Nymph

Step 3. Use a toothpick to spread 5-minute epoxy over the top and sides of the body to form the shellback. Then tip the fly upside down and let the epoxy dry, this will form a slight hump on the top and also keep the epoxy out of the legs.

Step 1. Mount a hook in the vise. Tie in the thread at the rear of the hook shank. Mount one end of the dubbing brush to the hook shank. Advance the thread to a little beyond the middle of the hook shank.

Step 2. Wrap the dubbing brush forward, preening back the fibers with each wrap. Continue wrapping the dubbing brush to the tie-off position; then secure it with 4 thread wraps and trim the excess. Advance the thread forward.

Step 3. Trim the body to shape. Dragon fly abdomens can be either long and cigar-shaped or short and squat.

Step 4. Mount the eyes behind the hook eye. Move the thread back to the front of the abdomen.

Step 5. Use the **side-lashed single-fiber legs** method (p. 37) to mount the rubber legs as shown. Leave the thread in front of the rear legs.

Step 6. Dub the thorax. Stack 2 hen feathers as shown, and coat them with Flexament.

Step 7. Mount the hen feathers, shiny side up, on top of the thorax as shown. Trim the excess stems.

Step 8. Dub over the thread wraps, and then between the eyes with figure-eight wraps to form a wide head. Tie off the thread and finish the head.

Strand Bodies—Krystal Flash

Krystal Flash Green Rock Worm

Originator: Rick Hafele
Hook: Nymph, 2X long, 2X heavy, size 12-18
Thread: Brown
Optional tail: Midge pupae, white Antron yarn fibers
Body: Peacock, green, (or color to match natural) Krystal Flash or Crystal Splash
Optional gills: Midge pupae, white Antron yarn fibers
Head: Brown dubbing, optional: black brass bead

Krystal Flash Mayfly Nymph

Hook: Nymph, 2X long, 2X heavy, sizes 14-20
Thread: Brown
Tail: Dark dun or brown hen feather fibers
Abdomen: Black Krystal Flash or golden-olive Crystal Splash
Wing case: Tag end of abdomen material
Thorax: Brown dubbing or brass bead
Optional hackle: Soft hackle, brown partridge or hen hackle

Note: Krystal Flash or other twisted Mylar is a wonderfully flashy body material for small nymphs. It is easy to wrap—even easier if you have a rotary vise—and it sinks without adding lead.

Krystal Flash Green Rock Worm

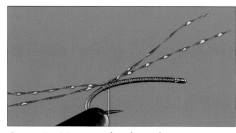

Step 1. Mount a hook in the vise. Tie in the thread at the front and using close, tight wraps move the thread to the rear. Mount 2-4 strands of Krystal Flash at the rear tie-in position.

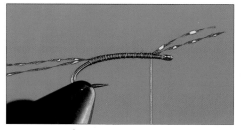

Step 2. To form a smooth underbody, use close tight wraps to bind down the tag ends of the Krystal Flash as shown. Trim the excess strands.

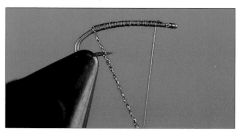

Step 3. Take the strands of Krystal Flash and twist them in counterclockwise direction to form a single tight strand. Without this twist, the Krystal Flash will flatten on the hook shank when wrapped and lose its characteristic sparkle.

Step 4. Using close tight wraps, wind the strand forward to the front of the body. Wrap the strand in layers to form a thicker or tapered body. Counter-twist the strand as needed. Secure the strand with 3-4 thread wraps and clip the excess.

Step 5. With a small amount of dubbing, dub the head. Tie off and finish the head.

Optional: K. F. Blood Worm

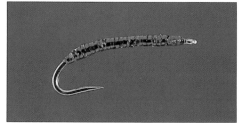

This fly has only a red Krystal Flash body; in hook sizes 10-14, it is a very good midge larva imitation for lakes or streams.

Optional: Black K. F. Midge

This pattern, in hook sizes 16-20, is a very good imitation of midge pupae found in streams; if more weight is needed, add a black metal bead to the fly as shown.

Optional: Gilled K. F. Midge Pupa

This midge pattern (hook sizes 10-16) is a good imitation of the large midges that occur in lakes. Black, green, golden-olive and red are the best colors.

Step 2. Mount 2-4 strands of Krystal Flash or Crystal Splash, and then advance the thread to the middle of the hook shank. Twist the strands together and wrap them over the thorax in layers to form a tapered body as shown.

Step 5. Pull the strands forward over the thorax, and use 3 thread wraps to secure them. Trim the excess strands, tie off the thread, and finish the head.

Step 1. Slide a Spirit River counterdrilled brass bead (with the small end forward) onto the hook. Mount the hook in the vise and form the body as shown above in Steps 1-4. Tie off, cut and cement the thread wraps.

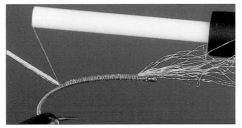

Step 1. Mount a hook in the vise. Tie in the thread behind the eye. Mount the Antron yarn at the front; then use the **shank wrap** method (p. 18) to secure the yarn to the top of the hook shank, and trim to length. Finish the fly as shown above.

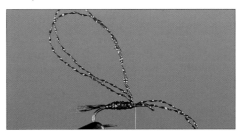

Step 3. Take the tag ends of the strands and double them over to form a loop. Take 2 thread wraps to secure the loop to the top of the hook shank as shown. Repeat this procedure—doubling over the loop strand and securing them—2 more times.

Optional: Bead Thorax K.F. Nymph

If a little more weight is needed for the fly, a bead may be added to the thorax area. Mount a bead as shown Step 1 of the option pattern. Complete the fly as shown above in Steps 1, 2, 3, and 5. For Step 4 push the bead back against the abdomen.

Step 2. Push the bead back over the front of the body. Tie in the thread in front of the bead, and build up a small thread taper to secure the bead as shown. Then dub the head, tie off the thread, and finish the head.

Krystal Flash Mayfly Nymph

Step 1. Mount the hook in the vise. Tie in the thread at the front and advance the thread to the rear tie-in position. Take 3-8 hen hackle fibers and mount them on top of the hook shank as shown. Then clip the excess.

Step 4. Dub the thorax area, stopping 4-5 thread wraps behind the hook eye.

Bead Thorax Soft Hackle

Krystal Flash is a good substitute, with more sparkle, for floss on soft-hackle flies, whether using a bead thorax (as shown) or a fur thorax. (See soft-hackle flies P. 68)

Chapter 4

Herl, Barb, Feather and Quill Bodies

The bodies in this chapter are formed from feathers or parts of feathers that are wrapped on the hook shank. They can be stripped to form a realistic segmented body or wrapped with the barbules attached to produce a lifelike movement when retrieved. With the many natural and dyed colors available, it is easy to match the color of any insect or to come up with your own color designs.

Herl, Barb, Feather and Quill Bodies—Ostrich Herl

R.C. Special

Originator: Steve Mayo
Hook: Nymph or scud, 2X heavy, sizes 6-20, weight optional
Thread: Red, or optional, olive
Shellback: Pearlescent tinsel or optional, olive latex strip
Optional rib: Scud, 2- 6-pound mono
Body: Ostrich herl, light gray or optional, olive
Note: This fly is a very effective sow bug imitation.

Ostrich Mayfly Nymph

Originator: Fred Arbona
Hook: Nymph, 2X heavy, 2X long, sizes 14-18, weighted
Thread: Olive or brown
Tail: Brown partridge hackle fibers
Rib: Optional, fine copper wire, counter-wrapped
Abdomen: Olive or brown ostrich herl
Wing case: Natural gray duck wing section
Thorax: Same as abdomen
Note: This simple, easily-tied fly is a good imitation for swimming mayfly nymphs.

R.C. Special

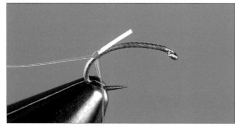

Step 1. Mount a hook in the vise. Tie in the thread at the front of the hook and wind to the rear. Mount a length of tinsel on top of the hook shank as shown. Then trim the excess tinsel.

Step 2. Mount 1-4 ostrich herls by their tips at the rear tie-in position as shown; then trim the excess herl. Advance the thread to the forward position.

Step 3. Wrap the herls forward with close, tight wraps and secure them with 3-4 thread wraps at the tie-off position. Then trim the excess herl.

Step 4. Fold the tinsel forward over the top of the hook shank and secure at the tie-off position as shown. Trim the excess tinsel, tie off the thread and finish the head.

Optional: Ostrich Scud

Originator: Fred Arbona. This is a simple, effective scud pattern. Tan and orange are good alternate colors.

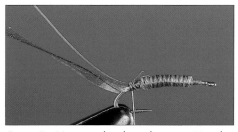

Step 1. Mount a hook in the vise. Use the **underbody direct wrap** method (p. 20) to weight the hook. Advance the thread to the rear. Taper one end of the latex strip, and mount it with the mono rib material at the rear tie-in position as shown.

Step 2. Mount the ostrich herl and wrap it forward. Pull the latex strip forward over the top of the hook shank and secure it with 3-4 thread wrap. Trim the excess latex.

Step 3. Wrap the mono over the body in evenly spaced wraps. When wrapping through the ostrich herl, rock the mono back and forth, to slide it between the barbules. Secure the mono, tie off the thread, and finish the head.

Ostrich Mayfly Nymph

Step 1. Mount the hook in the vise. Use the **underbody direct wrap** method (p. 20) to weight the thorax area of the hook shank. Advance the thread to the rear. Mount the partridge fibers on top of the hook shank and trim the excess.

Step 2. Mount the ostrich herl at the rear tie-in position and trim the excess. Wind the thread forward to the middle of the hook shank.

Step 3. Wrap the ostrich herl forward and secure at the tie-off position as shown. Do not cut the excess herl.

Step 4. Cut a section from a duck wing that is wide enough to cover the thorax and coat it with Flexament. When dry, mount the section, with the dark side down, at the tie-in position shown. Advance the thread to the front of the hook.

Step 5. Wrap the ostrich herl over the thorax area and secure it with 3-4 thread wraps. Trim the excess herl.

Optional: Ribbed Ostrich Mayfly Nymph

Step 6. Pull the wing section forward over the thorax and secure it with 3-4 thread wraps. Trim the excess fibers, tie off the thread, and finish the head.

To make the fly more durable and to add a little flash, a wire rib can be added to the fly.

Step 1. Follow Steps 1-3 above, but add a length of wire after tying in the tail fibers. After forming the abdomen, counter-wrap the wire over it. Secure the wire and trim the excess. Then finish the fly as shown above in Steps 4-6.

Herl, Barb, Feather and Quill Bodies—Biot

Biot Midge

Hook: Nymph or scud, 2X heavy, #14-#20
Thread: Black or dark brown
Abdomen: Black, brown, or olive biot
Optional wing case/gills: Pupa, light gray Antron
  yarn
Thorax: Peacock herl
Head: Optional, brass bead

Biot Caddis Pupa

Hook: Nymph or scud, #14-#16, weighted
Thread: Brown
Optional tail: Mayfly nymph, hen hackle fibers, brown
  or color to match abdomen
Abdomen: Biot, olive, tan, or brown
Optional wing case: Mayfly nymph, turkey wing
  section, coated with head cement.
Thorax: Dubbing to match color of abdomen.
Wing buds: Natural dun biots cut to shape
Legs: Light dun CDC fibers
Head: Optional, brass bead

Note: Biots used in fly tying come from the leading edges of flight feathers from turkeys, geese and ducks. Commercially dyed biots are often brittle; you can soak them in water before wrapping to prevent them from splitting when wrapped. Biots form attractive bodies for smaller flies.

Biot Midge

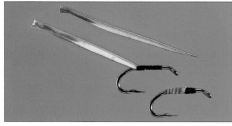

To form a smooth body, pull the biot from the feather or biot strip and mount it on the side of the hook shank with the notch facing down as shown. If the biot was cut from the strip, mount it so the convex side faces you.

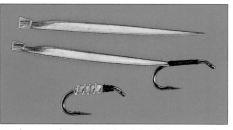

To form a fringed ribbed body, mount the pulled biot with the notch facing up. If the biot was cut from the stem, mount it so the concave side faces you.

Step 1. Mount a hook in the vise. Tie in the thread at the front and advance the thread to the rear tie-in position. Mount a biot by the tip with the notch facing down for a smooth body. Then wind the thread to the position shown.

Step 2. Use hackle pliers to clip (straight on) the butt of the biot; then take one wrap around the rear thread wraps. Overlap the next wrap to cover the fringed leading edge of the biot to form the smooth body. Continue wrapping forward.

Step 3. Use 3 thread wraps to secure the biot, and then cut the excess. Mount a peacock herl at the tie-in position.

Step 4. Wrap the herl forward and secure it with 3 thread wraps. Then tie off and finish the head.

Optional: Biot Midge Pupa

Use the beadhead version to fish deep and the unweighted version to fish shallow.

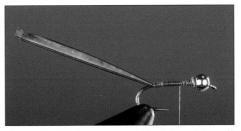

Step 1. Slide counterdrilled bead (small end forward) on the hook and secure it using the **bead head** method (p. 51). Advance the thread to the rear, and mount the biot with the notch facing up. Wind the thread forward as shown.

Step 2. To form a ribbed body, do not wrap over the expose the fringe. Wind the biot forward forming even, fringed spirals. Secure it at the tie-off position and trim the excess. Mount the Antron yarn and trim the excess as shown.

Step 3. Mount the peacock herl and wrap it over the thorax area. Secure it and trim the excess. Pull the Antron forward and secure it behind the bead. Tie off the thread behind the bead and cement the thread wraps. Trim the Antron to size.

Biot Caddis Pupa

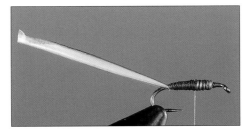

Step 1. Mount a hook in the vise. Use the **lead underbody** (p. 20) or beadhead method to weight the thorax. Wind the thread to the rear and mount a biot with the notch facing up. Then use the thread to form a smooth tapered underbody as shown.

Step 2. Wrap the biot forward and secure it with 3 thread wraps. Then dub the thorax area as shown.

Optional: Biot Mayfly Nymph

Step 3. Mount a biot on each side of the hook shank and trim to shape as shown in Step 4.

Step 4. Use the **bundled-fiber throat legs** method (p. 38) to mount the CDC fibers to the bottom of the hook shank as shown. Then use a little dark brown dubbing to dub the head. Tie off the thread and finish the head.

Step 1. Mount the hook in the vise. Form a lead underbody with a thread taper to the rear. For the tail, mount the hen hackle fibers. Mount the biot, notch up, and wrap it forward. Then mount the turkey wing section shiny side down.

Step 2. Dub the thorax area; pull the wing case forward over the dubbing and secure with 3 thread wraps.

Step 3. Trim the excess turkey feather fibers, tie off the thread, and finish the head. Then use a dubbing teaser to pick out the bottom of the thorax dubbing to form the legs.

Herl, Barb, Feather and Quill Bodies—Peacock Herl

Leadwing Coachman, Nymph

Hook: Nymph, 2X heavy, 2X long, sizes 10-14, weighted
Thread: Black
Tail: Brown hen hackle tip
Optional tag: Wet fly, fine gold tinsel
Body: Peacock
Throat: Brown hackle fibers
Optional hackle: Wet fly, brown hen
Wing case: Brown mallard shoulder feather, trimmed short
Optional wing: Wet fly, natural gray duck quill

Prince Nymph

Originator: Doug Prince
Hook: Nymph, 2X heavy, 2X-3X long, sizes 6-14, weighted
Thread: Black
Tail: Brown goose biots
Rib: Fine gold tinsel
Body: Peacock herl
Wings: White goose biots
Hackle: Brown
Head: Optional, brass bead

Note: Peacock bodied flies have long been a favorite of fly tiers. The flies shown here are good searching patterns. The Prince nymph works very well on rivers that have hatches of black caddis.

Leadwing Coachman

The most desirable peacock herl for wrapping bodies has dense barbules with a thin, narrow quill. These herls are found on peacock eye feathers, from the base of the eye down 2-3 inches.

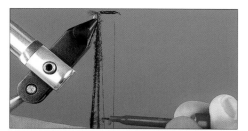

Step 1. Mount a hook in the vise. Use the **underbody direct wrap** method (p. 20) to weight the body. Wrap the thread to the rear and mount the hackle tip as shown.

Step 2. Mount 2-4 herls, a short distance back from their tips, at the tie-in position. Then trim the excess.

Step 3. Use the **dubbing loop** method (p. 28) to form a thread loop that is as long as the herl; wrap the thread forward. Gather the herl and thread together, draw them downward, and grip them with hackle pliers. The E-Z Hook shown here works well.

Step 4. Use the hackle pliers to gently spin the herls in a clockwise direction to form a fuzzy chenille next to the hook shank as shown. Do not spin the herl too tight or you may break one or more of the strands.

Step 6. Wrap the herl forward 1-3 wraps; then twist the herl clockwise to form the fuzzy chenille again. Continue this short wrap-and-spin cycle until the body is wrapped. Secure the herls with 3 thread wraps and trim the excess.

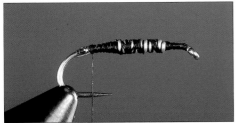

Step 7. Use the **bundled-fiber throat legs** method (p. 38) to mount the hen hackle fibers on the bottom of the hook shank. Then prepare a mallard shoulder feather as shown.

Step 8. Use the **slide mount** method (p. 18) to mount the feather with the curved side down. Then pull the feather stem back to the desired length, as shown. Trim the excess, tie off the thread, and finish the head.

Optional: Leadwing Coachman, Wet Fly

This fly is both an effective searching pattern and a good imitation of a drowned caddis adult.

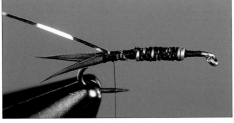

Step 1. Mount the hook and form the weighted underbody as shown above in Step 1. Then mount the tinsel at the rear and take 2-3 wraps forward. Secure the tinsel and trim the excess.

Prince Nymph

Step 2. Mount the peacock herl and form the body as shown above in Steps 2-5. Using the **collar hackle** method (p. 46), mount the hackle and take 2-3 wraps of the hackle. Secure the hackle with 3 thread wraps, and trim the excess.

Step 3. Use the **quill wing** methods (p. 42) to prepare and mount the wings as shown. Trim the excess quill, tie off the thread, and finish the head.

Step 1. Mount a hook in the vise and form the weighted underbody as shown above in Step 1. Use the **split tail** method (p. 25) to mount the biots at the rear tie-in position. Mount the rib tinsel and trim the excess.

Optional: B. H. Prince Nymph

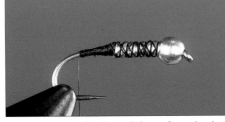

Step 2. Form the body as shown above in Steps 2-5. Counter-wrap the rib over the body. Use the **collar hackle** method (p. 46) to prepare, mount the hackle, and take 2-3 wraps of hackle. Secure the hackle and trim the excess.

Step 3. Mount 2 biots on top of the hook shank as shown. Then trim the excess, tie off the thread, and finish the head.

When a little more weight and sparkle is needed, a brass bead turns this fly into a great searching pattern.

Step 1. Use the **bead head** method (p. 51) to mount the bead and form the under-body.

Step 2. Finish the fly as shown above. Then use a small amount of peacock-colored dubbing and dub over the thread wraps as shown. Tie off and cut the thread behind the bead and cement the thread wraps.

Herl, Barb, Feather and Quill Bodies—Peacock Quill

Peacock Midge

Originator: Vic Bergman
Hook: Scud, 2X heavy, sizes 12-20
Thread: Black
Tail: Grizzly hackle fibers
Abdomen: 1 strand stripped peacock herl
Thorax: Natural ostrich herl, optional, brass bead
Hackle: Grizzly

Black Quill

Hook: Nymph 2X heavy, 2X long, sizes 10-16, weighted
Thread: Black
Tail: Medium dun hen hackle fibers
Abdomen: Stripped peacock herl
Wing case: Dark turkey feather section
Thorax: Gray dubbing

Note: Peacock herls from the eye and sword feathers produce the best stripped quills. On eyed feathers, the herls from the lower half of the eye have a two-tone color that produces a distinct banding when wrapped, but these herls are short and thin and are best for smaller flies. Herls from sword feathers are longer but more uniform in color; they work well for larger flies. Presoaking herls in water makes them more pliable and less likely to split when wrapped.

Peacock Midge

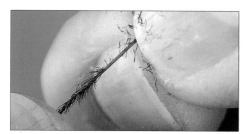

To remove the barbules from herl with your thumbnail, use light strokes and scrape the herl "against the grain" with your thumbnail, as shown.

Another way to remove the barbules is to use a coarse ink eraser. Hold the herl by its tip on a smooth hard surface and rub the eraser from tip to butt.

Step 1. Mount a hook in the vise. Tie in the thread at the front and advance it to the rear. Mount the hackle fibers at the rear tie-in position with 3 thread wraps. Do not trim the excess hackle fibers.

Step 2. Use 3 tight thread wraps to mount the stripped peacock herl back from the tip at the angle shown. Do not trim the excess.

Step 3. Counter-twist the thread to flatten it; then wrap the thread forward over the butt ends of the tail fibers and quill, forming a smooth underbody, as shown.

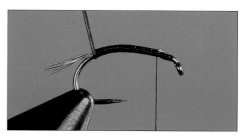

Step 4. Trim the excess quill and tail fibers. If the quill is short, use hackle pliers to grip it. Start by taking the first wrap of the quill toward the rear to cover the thread wraps.

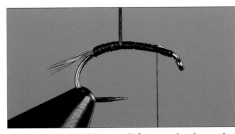

Step 5. Wind the quill forward. Place the wraps snug against one another, as shown. Do not overlap the edges or the segmented effect will be lost.

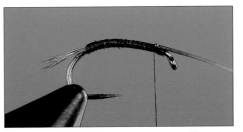

Step 6. Continue winding the quill to the front tie-off position and secure the quill with 3 thread wraps.

Step 7. Trim the excess quill. Mount the ostrich herl at the tie-in position; take 3-4 wraps forward and secure the herl with 3 thread wraps.

Optional: Beaded Peacock Midge

Step 8. Trim the excess herl. Use the **collar hackle** method (p. 47) to mount the feather and take 1-2 wraps; secure the hackle and trim the excess. Tie off the thread and finish the head.

When a little more weight and flash is needed, add a bead to the thorax.

Step 1. Slide the small-diameter end of a Spirit River counterdrilled bead onto the hook. Mount the hook in the vise. Tie in the thread behind the bead, as shown, and advance the thread to the rear.

Step 2. Form the tail and abdomen as shown above in Steps 1-6. Use a small amount of peacock dubbing and dub a small ball over the end of the abdomen. Tie off and cut the thread. Coat the thread wraps with head cement.

Step 3. Push the bead to the rear, against the dubbing ball. Tie in the thread in front of the bead and form a small thread bump in front of the bead to secure it. Then finish the fly as shown above in Steps 7-8.

Step 1. Mount a hook in the vise. Use the **underbody direct wrap** method (p. 20) to form tapered underbody. Mount the tail fibers and quill, and then form the abdomen as shown above. To reinforce the quill, coat it with a drop of CA glue.

Step 2. Prepare a feather section as wide as the hook gap and coat it with Flexament. Mount the feather section at the tie-in position. Wind the thread 2-3 wraps back over the abdomen. Trim the excess feather.

Step 3. Dub the thorax area, stopping 3-5 thread wraps behind the hook eye.

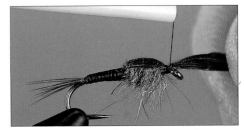

Step 18. Pull the feather section forward over the top of the thorax and secure it with 3 thread wraps. Trim the excess, tie off the thread, and finish the head. Then pick out the dubbing on the underside of the thorax.

Herl, Barb, Feather and Quill Bodies—Pheasant Tail Barbs

Pheasant Tail Nymph

Originator: Frank Sawyer/Al Troth
Hook: Nymph, 2X heavy, 2X long, sizes 12-20, weighted
Thread: Brown
Tail: Ring-necked pheasant tail barbs (barbs are called fibers by many tiers)
Rib: Copper wire, counter-wrapped
Abdomen: Ring-necked pheasant tail barbs
Wing case: Ring-necked pheasant tail barbs, optional, epoxy coated
Thorax: Peacock herl, optional brass bead
Legs: Ring-necked pheasant tail barbs
Head: Optional, brass bead

Flashback Pheasant Tail Nymph

Hook: Nymph, 2X heavy, 2X long, sizes 10-18, weighted
Thread: Brown
Tail: Ring-necked pheasant tail barbs, natural or olive
Shellback: Pearl Flashabou
Rib: Copper wire, counter-wrapped
Abdomen: Ring-necked pheasant tail barbs, natural or olive
Thorax: Peacock herl
Legs: Ring-necked pheasant tail barbs, natural or olive
Head: Optional, brass bead

Note: This fly pattern is one of the best mayfly nymph imitations in the history of fly fishing, and it catches as many trout now as it did in the past.

Pheasant Tail Nymph

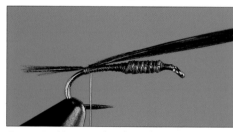

Step 1. Mount a hook in the vise. Use the **underbody direct wrap** method (p. 20) to weight the thorax area. Advance the thread to the rear. Align the tips of 6-8 pheasant tail barbs and mount them at the rear tie-in position. Do not cut the excess.

Step 2. Fold back the barbs back and mount a length of copper wire in front of the tail thread wraps. Then advance the thread to middle of the hook shank as shown.

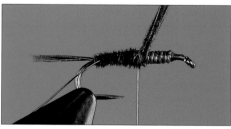

Step 3. Gather the barbs together and wrap them forward to the tie-off position. Secure them with 3 thread wraps.

Step 4. Trim the excess barbs. Counter-wrap the copper wire and secure it in front of the abdomen; then cut the excess wire. Prepare 8-12 barbs and measure them to the length of the hook shank by holding them in your right fingers as shown.

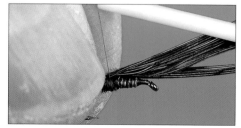

Step 5. Transfer the barbs to your left fingers, pinching them at the measured length. Use the **pinch wrap** method (p. 18) to mount the barbs with their butt ends over the front of the abdomen, as shown.

Step 6. Trim the excess barbs. Mount 2 peacock herls back about 1/2 inch from their tips; trim the excess. Use the **loop twisted** method (p. 34) to form a chenille; wrap it over the thorax, stopping 4-6 thread wraps behind the hook eye and trim the excess.

Step 7. Gather the barbs, pull them forward over the thorax, and secure them with 3 thread warps.

Step 8. On each side of the hook shank, fold 3-5 barb tips back and take a 2-3 thread wraps to secure them. Trim the excess barbs, tie off the thread, and finish the head.

Optional: Epoxy Back P. T. Nymph

For a more durable and shiny wing case, coat it with 5-Minute Epoxy.

Optional: Bead Head P. T. Nymph

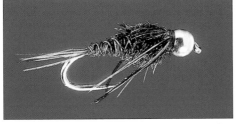

If a little more weight and flash is desired a brass bead may be added to the head.

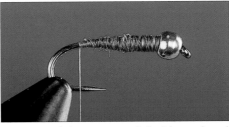

Step 1. Slide a counterdrilled brass bead on the hook with the small end toward the eye. Mount the hook in the vise. Use the **bead head** method (p. 51) to secure the head as shown. Then complete the fly as shown in the steps above.

Thorax Bead P. T. Nymph

On smaller hook sizes a bead head may be too large, but a brass bead can be used for the thorax to give the fly added weight and sparkle.

Flashback Pheasant Tail Nymph

Step 1. Slide a counterdrilled brass bead on the hook with the small end toward the eye. Mount the hook in the vise. Tie the fly following Steps 1-5. Tie off, cut thread, and cement the thread wraps.

Step 2. Push the bead back against the abdomen. Tie in the thread in front of the bead and build a small bump against it to hold it in place. Then follow Steps 7, 8 to finish tying the fly. For durability, coat the top of the wing case with 5-Minute Epoxy.

Step 1. Mount the hook and weight it as shown above. At the rear tie-in position, mount 5-10 barbs, 5-10 strands of Flashabou, and a length of copper wire. Advance the thread to the middle of the hook shank.

Step 2. Follow the steps above and complete the abdomen. Gather the Flashabou, pull it forward and secure it with 3 thread wraps. Counter-wrap the copper wire over the abdomen as shown.

Step 3. Secure the wire and trim the excess. Mount the peacock and wrap the thorax as shown above. Pull the Flashabou over the thorax and secure it with 3 thread wraps.

Step 4. Trim the excess Flashabou. Use the **bundled-fiber legs** method (p. 37) to mount 3-6 barbs on each side of the hook as shown. Trim the excess barbs. Tie off the thread and finish the head.

Herl, Barb, Feather and Quill Bodies—Marabou

Marabou P. T. Nymph

Hook: Nymph, 2X heavy, 2X long, sizes 10-16, weighted
Thread: Brown
Tail: Three pheasant tail fibers, natural or dyed to match body
Optional shellback: Thin Skin strip, olive, brown or black
Rib: Copper wire
Abdomen: Marabou fibers, olive, brown, or color to match natural
Wing case: Pheasant tail fibers, same color as tail
Thorax: Peacock herl
Legs: Pheasant tail fiber tips from wing case

Marabou Damsel

Hook: Nymph, 2X heavy, 2X-3X long, sizes 8-14, weight optional
Thread: Olive
Tail: Olive or brown marabou
Rib: Fine copper wire
Abdomen: Olive or brown marabou
Wing case: Olive or brown goose feather section
Thorax: Olive or brown marabou
Eyes: Green, red, or black mono

Note: The fluffy characteristic of marabou feathers gives flies a lifelike movement when retrieved through stillwaters or drifted in streams. Select marabou feathers that have long, dense barbules that extend to the end of the barbs.

Marabou P. T. Nymph

Step 1. Mount a hook in the vise. Use the **underbody lead direct wrap** method (p. 20) to add weight to the hook shank. Advance the thread to the rear. Mount 3 pheasant tail fibers at the rear tie-in position and trim the excess.

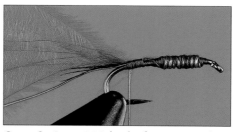

Step 2. Strip 4-10 barbs from a marabou feather. Mount the bundle of barbs a short distance back from their tips. Mount a length of copper wire at the tie-in position. Trim the excess barbs and wire.

Step 3. Advance the thread to the middle of the hook shank. Gather the barbs and grip them with hackle pliers. Gently twist the bundle of barbs clockwise to consolidate them. Wrap the barbs to the forward tie-off position.

Step 4. Secure the barbs with 3-4 thread wraps and trim the excess. Counter-wrap the copper wire forward, in evenly spaced wraps, to the forward tie-off position. Rock the wire back and forth while wrapping it to help release any trapped barbules.

Step 5. Secure the wire and trim the excess. Select and align the tips of 8-12 pheasant tail barbs. With your right fingers measure them to the length of the hook shank as shown.

Step 6. Transfer the bundle to your left fingers, pinching them at the measured length. Use the **pinch wrap** method (p. 18) to mount the barbs on top of the hook shank at the tie-in position.

Step 7. Trim the excess barbs. Mount 2 peacock herls a short distance back from their tips, then trim the excess. Use the **loop twisted** method (p. 34) to form a chenille, and wrap the thorax area. Secure the peacock behind the hook eye.

Step 8. Trim the excess peacock herl. Gather the pheasant barbs and pull them forward over the thorax. Secure them with 3 thread wraps at the tie-off position.

Step 9. Divide the barb tips and fold them back along the sides. Take 3 thread wraps over them to hold them in position. Tie off the thread and finish the head.

Optional: Shellback Marabou Nymph

A shellback is used to make the fly more realistic. For a flashier pattern, use Mylar tinsel for the shellback.

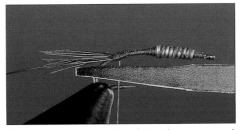

Step 1. Mount a hook in the vise and mount the weight, tail, and copper wire as shown above. Cut a strip of Thin Skin (or use any other latex substitute) as wide as the hook gap and at least twice as long as the hook shank. Taper one end.

Step 2. Mount the tapered end of the latex strip—shiny side up—at the rear tie-in position and wind the thread back to the rear thread wraps.

Marabou Damsel

Step 3. Mount the marabou barbs and form the abdomen as shown in Steps 2-4. Pull the latex strip over the abdomen and secure at the tie-off position. Do not trim the excess. Counter-wrap the copper wire, secure it, and trim the excess.

Step 4. Fold the latex back; take 3-4 thread wraps over the fold. Form the thorax as shown in Steps 4, 7, 8. Pull the latex forward, secure it, and trim the excess. Use the **bundled-fiber leg** method (p. 37) to mount 3-6 fibers per side. Finish the fly.

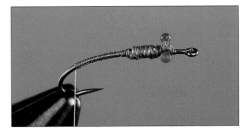

Step 1. Mount a hook in the vise. Use the **eye making** and **mounting** methods (p. 49) to mount the eyes 4-6 thread wraps behind the hook eye. Use the **underbody direct wrap** method (p. 20) to weight the body. Advance the thread to the rear.

Step 2. Use the **preparing feathers** methods (p. 22) to gather and align the tips on bunch of marabou. Extend the marabou tips one body length past the tie-in position and mount them. Mount a length of wire. Advance the thread to the tie-off position.

Step 3. Form and rib the abdomen as shown above in Steps 3-4; do not trim the excess barbs. Prepare a feather section that is as wide as the hook gap and mount it at the tie-in position. Advance the thread to the front of the eyes.

Step 4. Gather the marabou barbs and without twisting them, wrap them forward to the eyes. Pull the butt ends forward between the eyes and secure them. Trim the excess barbs. Pull the feather section forward, secure it, and finish the fly.

Herl, Barb, Feather and Quill Bodies—Clipped feathers

LaFontaine's Cased Caddis

Originator: Gary LaFontaine
Hook: Nymph, 2X heavy, 2X-3X long, sizes 8-14, weighted
Thread: Brown
Case: 2-3 brown, gray, or tan hen, grouse, or partridge feathers
Body: Pale yellow or bright green dubbing
Legs: Dark brown hen hackle fibers

Henry's Dragon Nymph

Originator: Henry Hoffman
Hook: Nymph, 2X-3X long
Thread: Olive or brown
Tail: Olive or brown Chickabou or hen feather tips
Rib: Copper wire
Body: 6-12 olive or brown Chickabou or hen feathers
Wing case: Turkey wing feather section
Legs: Chickabou feather tips
Eyes: Brass or lead
Thorax/head: Dubbing, color to match body

Note: Wrapped, clipped feathers are ideal for forming bulky bodies that are lightweight and durable. Any feather will work for this type of body, but soft-fibered feathers, even when clipped short, make a soft, pliable body that pulsates when moved through the water.

LaFontaine's Cased Caddis

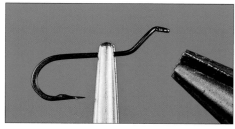

Step 1. Use two pairs of pliers to bend the front 1/3 of the hook shank up at a 45-degree angle.

Step 2. Mount the hook in the vise. Use the **underbody direct wrap** method (p. 20) to weight the rear portion of the hook as shown. Advance the thread to the rear tie-in position.

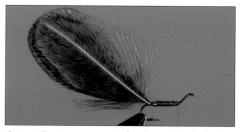

Step 3. Prepare 2 feathers (p. 21) that are the same size, place them together, and mount them by their butt ends at the rear tie-in position. Advance the thread to the forward tie-off position as shown.

Step 4. With hackle pliers, grip both feather tips and wind them forward to the tie-off position.

Step 5. Secure the feathers with 4 thread wraps and trim the excess. Trim the feathers into a roughly cylindrical shape, tapered to the rear as shown.

Step 6. Wind the thread forward to the hook eye and then back to the front of the case to form a thread base on the hook shank. Dub up the hook shank, using tightly spun dubbing, to form the body.

Henry's Dragon Nymph

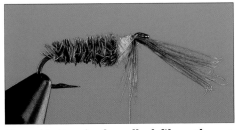

Step 7. Use the **bundled-fiber throat legs** method (p. 38) to mount the hen fibers on the bottom of the hook shank. Trim the excess fibers, tie off the thread, and finish the head.

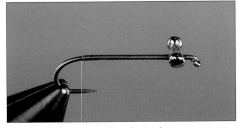

Step 1. Mount a hook in the vise. Tie in the thread behind the hook eye and wind back 10 thread wraps. Then use **eye mounting** method (p. 50) to mount the eyes on top of the hook shank. Wrap the thread to the rear tie-in position.

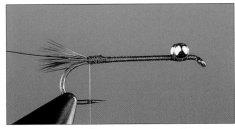

Step 2. Use the **preparing feathers** method (p. 21) to align and strip the feather fibers for the tail. Mount the fibers on top of the hook shank at the rear tie-in position and trim the excess. Mount a length of copper wire and trim the excess.

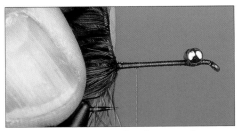

Step 3. Prepare 2 feathers and mount them as shown above in Step 3. Wind the thread forward. With hackle pliers, grip both feather tips and wind them forward with close, tight wraps, preening the barbs back with each wrap, as shown, to form a dense hackle.

Step 4. Secure the feathers and trim the excess. Repeat Step 3 until the full length of the abdomen is covered with dense hackle wraps.

Step 5. Trim the hackles flat to the height of the eyes on the top and bottom. Trim the sides to the width of the eyes. Taper the sides to the rear and round off the corners. Counter-wrap the wire and trim the excess.

Step 6. Remount the hook in the vise with the point up as shown.

Step 7. Dub the thorax behind the eyes as shown.

Step 8. Use the **bundled-fiber legs** method (p. 37) to mount the legs as shown.

Step 9. Trim the excess leg fibers. Dub the thorax, and dub around the eyes with figure-eight wraps. Position the thread as shown. Cut a wing feather section that is as wide as the abdomen and shape it. Coat the wing case with Flexament and let it dry.

Step 10. With 4 tight thread wraps, mount the wing case as shown and trim the excess.

Step 11. Place a small amount of dubbing on the thread and dub over the wing-case thread wraps; continue the wraps forward to the hook eye. Tie off, cut the thread, and finish the head.

Chapter 5

Dubbed Bodies

Dubbing is the material most often used in forming nymph bodies, and for good reasons. Dubbing is readily available in both natural and synthetic form; its textures range from coarse to fine; and it comes in a wide range of colors that can be mixed into an unlimited number of shades. By learning a few basic dubbing techniques shown in Chapter 1, you can dub almost any style and shape of nymph body.

Dubbed Bodies—Direct Dubbing—Long Fibers, Brushed

Dubbed Leech

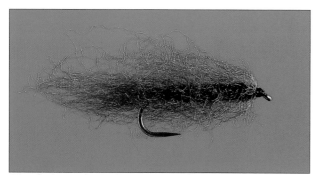

Hook: Nymph, 2X heavy, 2X-3X long, sizes 6-12, weighted
Thread: Black or color to match body
Tail: Fibers from material used for body
Body: Brown, olive, or black long-fiber yarn dubbing
Head: Optional, brass or colored bead

Dubbed Scud

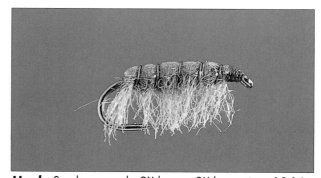

Hook: Scud or nymph, 2X heavy, 2X long, sizes 10-16, weighted
Thread: Olive or tan
Rib: Fine wire or 4- 6-pound mono
Shellback: Olive, or tan latex or plastic strip
Body: Olive or tan yarn dubbing

Note: Both natural and synthetic materials can be used for these flies; the only requirement is that the dubbing material be long enough to brush out and produce a halo effect around the hook shank.

Dubbed Leech

Step 1. To make the long-fiber dubbing needed for this fly, comb out a length of yarn and cut it into 3/4 to 1-inch lengths. Then mix the fibers together with you fingers.

Step 2. Mount a hook in the vise. Use the **underbody direct wrap** method (p. 20) to weight the hook. Advance the thread to the rear of the hook. Take a small bunch of the dubbing material used for the body and comb it out as shown.

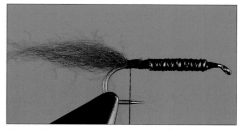

Step 3. Extend the material one shank-length behind the tie-in position, and mount it to the top of the hook shank. Trim the excess tail material.

Step 4. Use the **direct dubbing** method (p. 27) to loosely apply the dubbing to 2-3 inches of thread. Do not over-spin the dubbing; instead form a loose noodle as shown.

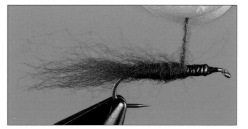

Step 5. Wind the material forward with close tight wraps, forming an even body as shown.

Step 6. If more dubbing is need, apply it as shown above in Step 2. Continue dubbing to within 2-4 thread wraps of the hook eye. Pull off any excess dubbing from the thread. Preen back the material and tie off the thread as shown.

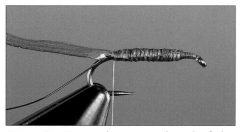

Step 7. Use a **dubbing tease**r (p. 29) to brush out the dubbing as shown.

B/H Dubbed Leach

If a little more flash or weight is desired for this pattern, use the **bead head** method (p. 51) to mount the bead of your choice.

Dubbed Scud

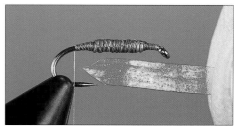

Step 1. Mount a hook in the vise. Use the **underbody direct wrap** method (p. 20) to the weight the body. Advance the thread to the rear. Cut a strip of latex that is as wide as the hook gap and taper one end as shown.

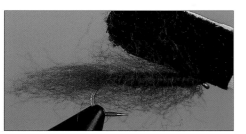

Step 2. Mount the tapered end of the latex strip on top of the hook shank at the rear tie-in position. Mount a length of wire on the near side of the hook shank at the rear tie-in position.

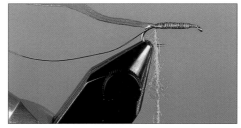

Step 3. Comb out a length of yarn and cut it into 1/2 to 3/4 inch lengths. Mix the fibers as shown in Step 1 of the previous sequence. Use the **direct dubbing** method (p. 27) to apply the dubbing to the thread as shown. Do not over-spin the dubbing.

Step 4. Wind the dubbing forward forming a body as shown. Stop 4-6 thread wraps behind the hook eye. Strip off the excess dubbing, preen the fibers back, and take 2 thread wraps around the hook shank.

Step 5. Use a dubbing teaser to brush out the fibers from the dubbed body as shown. Do not over-tease the dubbing; just brush out enough fibers to form the legs.

Step 6. Preen the brushed-out fibers from the top and sides down with your left fingers. Us your right fingers to pull the latex strip forward over the top of the body. Use 4 tight thread wraps to secure the latex.

Step 7. Trim the excess latex. Wind the wire forward with evenly spaced wraps. Rock the wire back and forth to slide it between the dubbing fibers. Secure the wire and trim the excess. Tie-off the thread and finish the head. Trim the legs as shown.

Dubbed Bodies—Direct Dubbing-Long Fibers, Brushed

Antron Caddis Pupa

Hook: Scud/shrimp, 2X heavy, sizes 10-14, weighted
Thread: Brown
Rib: Tan or cream long-fiber Antron dubbing
Abdomen: Brown or green Larva Lace or other plastic tubing
Wing case: Dark brown or black Antron yarn
Thorax: Brown Hare-Tron dubbing
Legs: Natural CDC fibers
Head: Brown dubbing, optional, brass bead

Boatman

Hook: Nymph, 2X long, 2X heavy, sizes 14-16, weighted
Thread: Tan
Shellback: Brown Thin Skin, or latex strip
Abdomen: White Antron dubbing, followed by tan or olive Antron dubbing
Legs: Goose biots or rubber legs, color to match body
Eyes: Mono
Thorax/head: Tan or olive Antron dubbing

Note: Both of these flies use long, brushed Antron dubbing fibers to imitate air bubbles trapped next to the body. It is a technique that can be easily adapted to other nymph or emerger patterns.

Antron Caddis Pupa

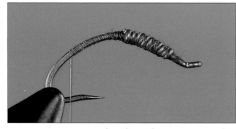

Step 1. Mount a hook in the vise. Use the **underbody direct wrap** method (p. 20) to weight the body as shown. Advance the thread to the rear.

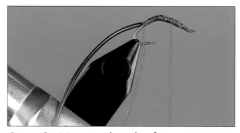

Step 2. Mount a length of Larva Lace at the rear tie-in position and trim the excess. Use the **dubbing loop** method (p. 28) to form a thread loop 4-5 inches in length at the rear tie-in position. Advance the thread forward as shown.

Step 3. Wind the Larva Lace forward to the tie-off position, leaving a small gap between each wrap. Secure the Larva Lace with 4 tight thread wraps, trim the excess, and bind down the tag end.

Step 4. Take a pinch of long fiber-dubbing. Apply it to the thread strands and spin it into a loose noodle as shown.

Step 5. Wind the dubbing strand forward in the gaps between the Larva Lace. Secure at the tie-off position and trim the excess.

Step 6. Use the dubbing teaser to brush out the fibers as shown. Trim any long fibers.

Step 7. Dub the thorax and use the **Antron wing bud** method (p. 44) to mount the wings on the sides of the thorax as shown.

Step 8. Use the **bundled-fiber throat legs** method (p. 38) to mount the legs on the bottom of the hook shank at the tie-in position. Trim the excess fibers. Dub over the thread wraps to form the head as shown. Tie off the thread, and finish the head.

Optional: B/H Antron Caddis Pupa

If more weight and flash is desired, use the **bead head** method (p. 51) in Step 1, and then complete the fly.

Boatman

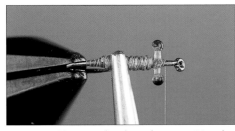

Step 1. Mount a hook in the vise. Use the **underbody direct wrap** method (p. 20) to weight the fly. Use the **eye making** and **mounting** methods (p. 49) and mount the eyes as shown. Then use smooth pliers to gently flatten the wire wraps.

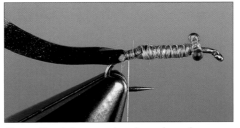

Step 2. Advance the thread to the rear. Cut a strip of Thin Skin that is as wide as the hook gap and taper one end. Mount the tapered end of the strip (with the shiny side up) at the rear tie-in position.

Step 3. Apply a small amount of white Antron dubbing to the thread and loosely spin it. Wind it over the rear of the hook shank forming a small ball of dubbing.

Step 4. Use the dubbing teaser to brush out the fibers; then preen them rearward and downward as shown. Trim any long fibers.

Step 5. Dub the abdomen so its width—when viewed from the top—is almost equal to the distance between the eyeballs. Lightly brush the dubbing on the bottom with the dubbing teaser as shown.

Step 6. Use the **side-lashed single-fiber legs** method (p. 37) to mount biots to the side of the hook shank as shown.

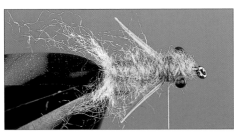

Step 7. Trim the excess biots. Dub over thread wraps, and dub between the eyes with figure-eight wraps to build up the head. Return the thread to the front of the legs.

Step 8. Pull the shellback over the top of the body and secure it with 3 loose thread wraps as shown. Tighten the thread just enough to form a shellback over the body that is about as wide as the eyes.

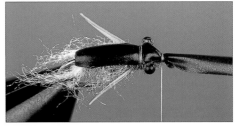

Step 9. Wind the thread forward to the front of the eyes. Pull the shellback forward and secure it with 4 tight thread wraps and trim the excess. Tie off the thread and finish the head.

Dubbed Bodies—Direct Dubbing, Loose Twist

Gold Ribbed Hare's Ear

Hook: Nymph, 2X heavy, 2X long, sizes 8-16, weighted
Thread: Brown
Tail: Hare's mask guard hairs, optional: mottled brown hen hackle fibers
Rib: Oval gold tinsel
Abdomen: Natural hare's ear dubbing
Wing case: Mottled turkey feathers, optional: pearl Flashabou
Thorax: Natural hare's ear dubbing, optional: dark hare's ear dubbing
Optional head: Brass bead

Bead Head Caddis Pupa

Hook: Nymph, 1X-2X heavy, 2X long, sizes 10-16
Thread: Brown
Tail: Mottled light brown hen hackle fibers
Rib: Fine gold tinsel
Abdomen: Natural tan Hare-Tron dubbing
Thorax: Brown Hare-Tron dubbing
Legs: Mottled light brown hen hackle fibers
Head: Brass bead

Note: When loosely twisted on the thread for dubbing, hare's mask with both underfur and guard hairs, and other similar furs, are ideal for forming shaggy bodies. It is a very fast way to make a bulky body on smaller hooks. The Gold Ribbed Hare's Ear is one of many good nymphs tied using this technique.

Gold Ribbed Hare's Ear

Step 1. Mount a hook in the vise. Use the **underbody direct wrap** method (p. 20) to weight the hook. Advance the thread to the rear. Select and cut a pinch of fur from the cheek area of the hare's mask and remove most of the underfur.

Step 2. Extend the guard hairs about 1/2 a hook shank-length behind the tie-in position, and mount the hairs to the top of the hook shank. Trim the excess and bind down tag ends; return the thread to the rear.

Step 3. At the rear tie-in position, mount a length of tinsel on top of the hook shank. Clip a bunch of fur from the hare's mask and mix it, or use the prepackaged variety. Twist the dubbing around the thread, tapering the strand at the top as shown.

Step 4. Wrap the dubbing forward, forming a tapered body. Stop at the middle of the hook shank, and remove any excess dubbing from the thread.

Step 5. Wind the ribbing forward with 3-5 evenly space wraps, and secure it with 4 tight thread wraps at the tie-off position. Trim the excess tinsel. Cut a section of turkey feather barbs the width of the hook gap and coat it with Flexament.

Step 6. Mount the feather section by its thick end at the tie-in position with the most distinctly marked side facing down. Take 2-3 thread wraps toward the rear, binding the feather section to the top of the abdomen as shown.

Optional: Gold Ribbed Hare's Ear

Tie the fly the same as shown above, but for the thorax use a darker hare's ear dubbing for a greater contrast in appearance.

Optional: B/H Olive Hare's Ear

Use the **bead head** method (p. 51) to mount a bead; then complete the fly as shown above. Dyed olive and brown are good optional colors for this pattern.

Step 7. Dub over the thorax stopping 4-5 thread wraps behind the hook eye. Pull the feather section forward over the thorax, and secure it behind the eye with 3-4 tight thread wraps. Trim the excess feather barbs. Then tie off the thread and finish the head.

Optional: Gold Ribbed Hare's Ear

Some tiers do not like to mess with hare's masks. A good option is to use hen feather barbs for the tail and prepackaged dubbing for the body. Natural Hare-Tron dubbing was used for this fly.

Optional: Flashback Hare's Ear

If a little flash is desired, replace the wing case feather section with pearl Flashabou.

Step 1. Mount a hook in the vise. Complete the fly as shown above in Steps 1-5. Mount 6-12 strands of pearl Flashabou at the tie-in position; wrap the thread back onto the abdomen as shown. Then finish the fly as shown above in Step 7.

B/H Flashback Hare's Ear

For a lot of flash and extra weight, use the **bead head** method (p. 51) to mount a bead on the hook; then complete the fly as shown above. This is a very good searching nymph pattern.

Bead Head Caddis Pupa

Step 1. Place a bead on the hook, and mount the hook in the vise. Use the **bead head** method (p. 51) to secure the bead and form the underbody. Advance the thread to the rear.

Step 2. Align and strip feather fibers for the tail. Extend the fibers about 1/2 the hook-shank length behind the tie-in position, and mount them to the top of the hook shank. Mount a length of tinsel at the tie-in position.

Step 3. Trim the excess tinsel and fibers. Dub the abdomen as shown above in Steps 3-4, stopping 10-12 thread wraps behind the bead. Wind the tinsel forward with 3-5 evenly spaced wraps; secure it and trim the excess.

Step 4. Use the **bundled-fiber legs** method (p. 37) to mount the aligned feather fibers on each side of the hook shank as shown.

Step 5. Trim the excess fibers. Dub the thorax. Tie off the thread behind the bead and cement the thread wraps.

Dubbed Bodies—Direct Dubbing, Tight Twist

TDC

Originator: Richard Thompson
Hook: Nymph, 2X heavy, 1X-2X long, sizes 12-16
Thread: Black
Rib: Fine silver tinsel
Abdomen: Black dubbing
Thorax: Black dubbing, optional: Spirit River counterdrilled metal bead
Head: White ostrich herl

King's Caddis Pupa

Originator: Matt King
Hook: Scud or pupa, sizes 8-16, weighted
Thread: Green or color to match dubbing
Shellback: Black Scud Back
Rib/gills: White ostrich herl, twisted with 2-pound mono
Abdomen: Green dubbing
Wing buds: Dark brown or dun hen feathers, burnt or cut to shape, and coated with Flexament
Legs: Olive CDC fibers
Antennae: 2 lemon woodduck barbs
Head: Dark brown dubbing

Note: These two patterns are good examples of tightly-twisted dubbed bodies; the midge pattern uses a soft-textured dubbing that gives the fly a smooth, tight body, while the caddis pattern uses a coarse-textured dubbing that gives the fly a rough tight body.

TDC

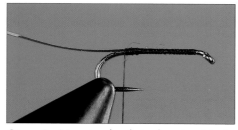

Step 1. Mount a hook in the vise. Tie in the thread at the front of the hook and advance it to the rear. Mount a length of tinsel on top of the hook shank at the rear tie-in position, and trim the excess.

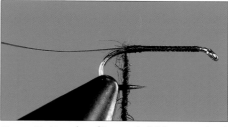

Step 2. Use the **direct dubbing** method (p. 27) to apply a pinch of dubbing on thread, then twist it clockwise into a tight cord as shown.

Step 3. Wind the dubbing forward, forming a smooth tapered body as shown. Remove any excess dubbing from the thread.

Step 4. Wind the tinsel forward, in 3-5 evenly spaced wraps. Secure the tinsel and trim the excess. Advance the thread forward 5-8 wraps. Mount the ostrich herl about 1 inch back from its tip and trim the excess.

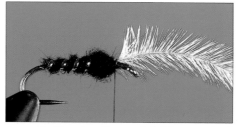

Step 5. Use the **direct dubbing** method (p. 27) to apply a small amount of dubbing onto the thread, and twist it into a tight cord. Then wind the dubbing over the thorax so that it is half again as wide as the body. Remove any excess dubbing from the thread.

Step 6. Wind the thread forward, stopping 3-4 thread wraps behind the hook eye. Wind the ostrich herl forward 4-6 turns and secure it at the tie-off position as shown. Trim the excess herl; tie off the thread and finish the head.

Optional: Bead Thorax TDC

Step 1. Slide the small-holed side of the bead onto the hook and mount the hook in the vise. Form the abdomen as shown above in Steps 1-4. Tie off the thread and cement the thread wraps.

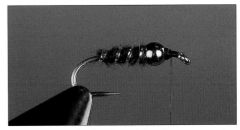

Step 2. Push the bead back against the abdomen. Tie in the thread in front of the bead. Build a small thread bump in front of the bead to secure it as shown. Then mount the ostrich herl and complete the fly.

King's Caddis Pupa

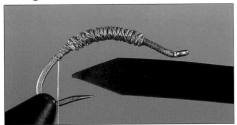

Step 1. Mount a hook in the vise. Use the **underbody direct wrap** method (p. 20) to weight the body. Advance the thread to the rear. Cut a strip of Thin Skin that is about as wide as the hook gap, and taper one end as shown.

Step 2. At the rear tie-in position, mount the tapered end of the strip with the shiny side facing up. Mount an ostrich herl 1/2 inch back from its tip, and length of 2-pound mono, at the rear tie-in position. Coat 3-4 inches of the hanging thread with tying wax.

Step 3. Use the **direct dubbing** method (p. 27) to apply the dubbing to the thread and twist the dubbing clockwise into a tight cord as shown.

Step 4. Wind the dubbing forward to form the body. If the dubbing cord loosens, pause and twist it tight again. Twist more dubbing onto the thread as is needed. Remove any excess dubbing from the thread.

Step 5. Pull the Thin Skin strip over the top of the body and secure it at the tie-off position and trim the excess. Gather the ostrich herl and mono and grip the ends with hackle pliers as shown.

Step 6. Gently twist the herl and mono clockwise into a chenille. Wind the herl forward with 6-8 evenly spaced wraps.

Step 7. Secure the herl and trim the excess. Use the **bundled-fiber throat legs** method (p. 38) to mount the CDC fibers. Trim the excess fibers. Then dub over the thread wraps as shown. Use a **wing feather** method (p. 41) to form the wings.

Step 8. Use the **slide mount** method (p. 18) to mount a wing on each side of the body as shown; trim the excess.

Step 9. Mount 2 woodduck feather barbs on top of the hook shank and trim the excess. Dub over the thread wraps. Tie-off the thread and finish the head.

Dubbed Bodies—Direct Dubbing, Tight and Loose Twist

Basic Mayfly Nymph

Hook: Nymph, 2X heavy, 1-3X long, sizes 8-18, weighted
Thread: Brown or color of choice
Tail: Hen feather fibers
Rib: Copper wire
Abdomen: Olive or brown fine dubbing
Wing case: Dark brown Antron yarn
Thorax: Brown or olive dubbing

General Mayfly Nymph

Hook: Nymph 2X heavy, 1X-3X long, sizes 8-18, weighted
Thread: Brown
Tail: Feather barbs
Rib: Copper wire
Shellback: Feather barbs, optional: Thin Skin or latex strip
Gills: Ostrich herl, optional: afterfeather
Abdomen: Olive dubbing
Wing case: Feather section coated with Flexament
Thorax: Olive dubbing
Optional legs: Hen feather

Note: On these mayfly nymph patterns, the tightly-twisted dubbing helps shape the abdomen, while the loosely-twisted dubbing used on the thorax gives them a rough, lifelike outline. Both of these flies are designed to show a number of options that will help you tie a mayfly nymph pattern to imitate any natural, by matching its size, shape, color, and any other characteristic features.

Basic Mayfly Nymph

Step 1. Mount a hook in the vise. Use the **underbody direct wrap** method (p. 20) to weight the body. Advance the thread to the rear. **Align and strip** (p. 21) 3-8 barbs; extend them 1/2 the shank-length behind the tie-in position; mount them.

Step 2. Trim the excess barbs. Mount a length of copper wire and trim the excess. Use the **direct dubbing** method (p. 27) to apply the dubbing to the thread, and then twist the dubbing clockwise into a tight cord as shown.

Step 3. Wrap the dubbing forward to the middle of the hook shank, forming a tapered body. Add dubbing as needed; if the dubbing cord loosens, twist it tight again.

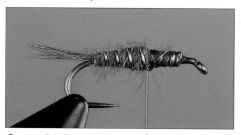

Step 4. Counter-wrap the copper wire with 4-6 evenly spaced wraps, and secure it at the tie-off position; trim the excess.

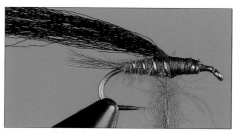

Step 5. Mount a length of yarn at the tie-in position and trim the excess. Bind the yarn 3-4 thread wraps back over the top of the abdomen. Dub the thread as shown in Step 2 and twist it counterclockwise into a loose cord as shown.

Step 6. Wind the dubbing forward, forming a thorax that is a little larger in diameter than the abdomen. Add more dubbing as needed. Stop 4-5 thread wraps behind the hook eye.

General Mayfly Nymph

Step 7. Pull the yarn forward and secure it with 3-4 thread wraps; trim the excess yarn. Tie off and finish the head. If the thorax is not roughly textured enough, use a dubbing teaser or bobbin to tease out the bottom fibers as shown.

Step 1. Mount a hook in the vise. Form the underbody as shown above in Step 1. Mount 3-6 feather barbs for the tail. Mount a length of copper and trim the excess. Mount an ostrich herl about 1/2 inch back from its tip and trim the excess.

Step 2. Cut a turkey feather section that is about 2/3 the width of the hook gap and coat the section with Flexament. Mount the section by the tip at the rear tie-in position; wind the thread to the rear thread wraps. Dub the abdomen as shown above in Steps 2-3.

Step 3. Use 4-6 evenly spaced wraps to wind the ostrich herl forward to the tie-off position. Secure the herl and trim the excess.

Step 4. Pull the feather section forward and secure it at the tie-off position. Counter-wrap the copper wire forward in 4-6 evenly spaced wraps and secure it at the tie-off position.

Step 5. Form the rest of the body as shown above in Steps 5-7.

Optional: Gilled Mayfly Nymph

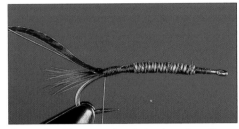

Step 1. Mount a hook in the vise. Form the underbody, mount the tails and wire as shown above. Cut a strip of Thin Skin 1/2 the width of the hook gap. Taper one end, and mount the tapered end with the shiny side up at the rear tie-in position.

Step 2. Select an aftershaft feather (use ostrich herl on smaller flies), that is a little wider than the hook gap; mount it about 1/2 inch back from its tip, on top of the hook shank at the rear tie-in position. Dub the abdomen as shown above.

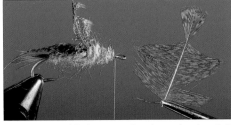

Step 3. Pull the feather forward and secure it at the tie-off position and trim the excess. Pull the strip forward and secure it. Wrap the copper wire forward in 4-8 evenly spaced wraps; secure the wire and trim the excess.

Step 4. Fold the strip back and take 3-5 thread wraps over the fold. Dub the thorax as shown above. Prepare a feather with barbs at least twice the width of the thorax, as shown. Mount the feather by the tip with the dull-side up. Trim the excess.

Step 5. Pull the feather forward, secure it, and trim the excess. Pull the strip forward, secure it, and trim the excess. Tie-off and finish the head. Note: a wide wing case will force the barbs down; trim the wing case it if you want to raise the legs.

Dubbed Bodies—Direct-Dubbed Loop

Basic Caddis Larva

Hook: Nymph or pupa, 2X heavy, 2X long, sizes 8-16, weighted
Thread: Brown
Optional gills: White ostrich herl, lashed
Abdomen: Olive dubbing
Legs: Feather fibers
Head: Brown dubbing, optional: bead head

Basic Caddis Pupa

Hook: Nymph or pupa, 2X heavy, 2X long, sizes 4-16, weighted
Thread: Brown
Gills: Ostrich herl, twisted with thread
Abdomen: Green dubbing
Thorax: Brown dubbing
Wing buds: Wing film or quill section cut to shape
Legs: Hen and CDC fibers
Head: Dubbing, optional: brass bead

Note: When used with a soft- to medium-textured dubbing, the direct-dubbed loop forms a tightly segmented body that is ideal for matching a caddis larva or pupa body. These patterns are designed to show a few of the options possible using this method. By changing the hook size and dubbing color, it is possible to match most caddis larvae and pupae.

Basic Caddis Larva

Step 1. Mount a hook in the vise. Use the **underbody direct wrap** method (p. 20) to weight the body. Advance the thread to the rear. Use the **direct dubbing** method (p. 27) to form an even dubbing cord on 2-4 inches of the thread.

Step 2. The size of the segment is determined by the amount of dubbing on the thread. Use a dubbing hook to catch the thread at the end of the dubbing strand; then double the thread back on itself and place the bobbin above the hook shank as shown.

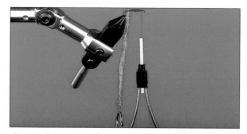

Step 3. Wrap the tying thread back to the dubbed thread to bind both ends of the loop to the hook shank. Then wind the thread forward to the front tie-off position.

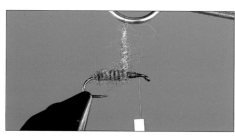

Step 4. Twist the dubbing hook in a clockwise direction to form a tight cord. Wrap the cord forward to the tie-off position and secure it with 3-4 thread wraps.

Step 5. Trim the excess dubbing cord. **Align and strip** (p. 22) 5-10 barbs from a feather. Use the **bundled-fiber throat legs** method (p. 38) to mount the barbs on the bottom of the hook shank. Trim the excess.

Step 6. Use the **direct dubbing** method (p. 27) to dub the head. Tie off the thread and finish the head.

Optional:
Bead Head Basic Caddis Larva

A bead will add a little flash and extra weight to the fly, while the lashed gills are used to add a realistic touch.

Step 1. Use the **bead head** method (p. 51) to mount the bead and form the underbody. Advance the thread to the rear. Mount an ostrich herl by its tip to the bottom of the hook shank and trim the excess. Form 3-4-inch **dubbing loop** (p. 28).

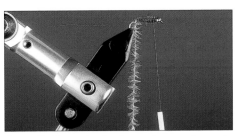

Step 2. Form the body as shown above in Steps 1-4. Cut the bottom end of the thread loop to form 2 thread strands. With hackle pliers, grip one thread strand and the ostrich herl and twist them into a chenille.

Step 3. Pull the herl forward along the bottom of the hook shank and secure it at the front tie-off position. Wind the second strand of thread forward between the body segments; secure it and trim the excess. Finish the fly as shown above in Steps 5-6.

Basic Caddis Pupa

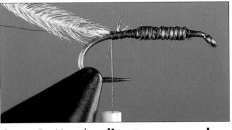

Step 1. Use the **direct wrap underbody** method (p. 20) to weight the fly. When mounting the tying thread leave a 5-inch thread tag at the rear tie-in position. Mount an ostrich herl one inch back from its tip and trim the excess.

Step 2. Form the abdomen as shown above in Step 1-4. Use hackle pliers to grip the ends of the thread strand and herl, and gently twist them together to form a chenille. Wrap the chenille forward between the body segments.

Step 3. Secure the herl and trim the excess. Use the direct dubbing method to dub the thorax area. Use the **cut wing** method (p. 39) to form wings that are as wide as the body.

Step 4. Place the wings over the top of the thorax and secure them; trim the excess. **Align and strip** (p. 22) 6-10 barbs from a hen feather; use the **bundle-fiber throat leg** method (p. 38) to mount them to the bottom of the hook shank, and trim the excess.

Step 5. Align and strip 8-12 CDC barbs from a feather; mount half of them on top of the hook shank and the other half on the bottom of the hook shank. Trim the excess.

Optional:
B/H Basic Caddis Pupa

Step 6. Use the **direct dubbing** method (p. 27) to dub the head. Tie-off the thread and finish the head.

Use the **bead head** method (p. 51) to form the underbody; then complete the fly as shown above. Tie off the thread behind the bead.

Dubbed Bodies—Trapped-Loop Dubbing

Basic Stone

Hook: Nymph, 2X heavy, 2X-3X long, sizes 4-14, weighted
Thread: Brown or black
Tail: Brown or black round rubber
Rib: Copper wire
Body: Golden brown to black dubbing
Wing case: Turkey feather section, coated with Flexament, optional: Brown Antron yarn
Legs: Brown or black round rubber
Optional head: Brass or black bead

General Stone

Hook: Nymph, 2X heavy, 2X-3X long, sizes 4-14
Thread: Black or brown
Tail: Black or brown goose biots
Rib: Black or brown vinyl ribbing
Body: Black to golden brown dubbing
Wing case/head: Cut turkey feather sections, cut to shape and coated with Flexament
Legs: Black or brown round rubber
Optional head: Black or brass bead
Antennae: Black or brown goose biots

Note: The trapped-loop method is a good way to form a large or bulky body from most dubbing materials, but this technique works especially well with the short, coarse dubbing that is often used for tying stonefly patterns. The fly patterns shown above were designed to show some of the options possible in tying a pattern to match the natural.

Basic Stone

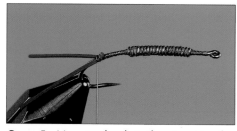

Step 1. Mount a hook in the vise. Use the **underbody direct wrap** method (p. 20) to weight the body. Advance the thread to the rear. Use **split tail** method (p. 25) to mount the rubber strand at the rear tie-in position.

Step 2. Mount a length of cooper wire at the rear tie-in position and trim the excess. Use the **dubbing loop** method (p. 28) to form 4- 6-inch loop. Advance the thread to the middle of the hook. Apply a thin coat of wax to one strand of the loop.

Step 3. Apply the dubbing in an even layer to the waxed thread. Do not overdub the loop. To form a neat, tight body, use a moderate amount of dubbing on the thread.

Step 4. Use a dubbing hook to catch the thread at bottom of the loop; carefully remove your fingers. Then use the hook to twist the trapped dubbing loop in a clockwise direction to compact the dubbing.

Step 5. Wind the dubbing loop forward, building a tapered abdomen with layers of dubbing. After wrapping the complete dubbing loop, secure it; form another dubbing loop and continue forming the abdomen, stopping at the shank midpoint.

Step 6. Secure the dubbing loop and trim the excess. Counter-wrap the wire in evenly spaced wraps; secure it and trim the excess. Mount the feather section at the tie-in position and bind it to the front of the abdomen. Trim the excess.

Step 7. Dub the thorax, stopping 6-8 thread wraps behind the hook eye. Wind the thread back to the middle of the thorax. Use the **side-lashed single-fiber leg** method (p. 37) to mount the legs. Dub over the thread wraps, continue to the front of the thorax.

Step 8. Pull the feather section forward and secure it with 3-4 tight thread wraps, and trim the excess. Tie off the thread and finish the head.

B/H Basic Stone

A bead can be used to add more weight and flash to the fly. Yarn can be used to build up the underbody on larger flies so that less dubbing is needed to tie the fly.

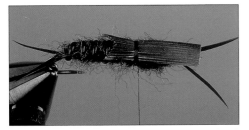

Step 1. Use the **bead head** method (p. 51) to mount the bead and weight the fly. Wrap yarn over the hook shank to form the **underbody** (p. 21) as shown. Then complete the fly. Tie off the thread behind the bead and cement the thread wraps.

General Stone

Step 1. Mount a hook in the vise. Use the **underbody direct wrap** method (p. 20) to weight the thorax. Use the **split tail** method (p. 25) to mount the biots at the front and rear of the hook shank. Mount a length of vinyl ribbing and trim the excess.

Step 2. Form the abdomen as shown above in Steps 2-6. Then wrap the vinyl ribbing, secure it and trim the excess. Dub the thorax area stopping 8-10 thread wraps behind the hook eye. Wind the thread back to the middle of the thorax.

Step 3. Use the **cut wing case** method (p. 39) to form 2 matching wing cases, each as wide as the hook gap or about 1 1/2 times the width of the thorax. Mount one wing case, centered on top of the hook shank as shown.

Step 4. Trim the tag end of the wing case. Use the **side-lashed single-fiber** method (p. 37) to mount the legs over the wingcase thread wraps.

Step 5. Dub over the thread wraps around the front legs. Mount the second wing case on the top of the hook shank and trim the excess. Advance the thread to just behind the hook eye. Prepare a feather section the width of the thorax as shown.

B/H General Stone

Step 6. Mount the thin end of the feather section at the front tie-in position as shown. Dub over the thread wraps forming the head, leaving the thread in the position shown.

Step 7. Fold the feather section back and secure it with 3-4 thread wraps and trim it as shown. Tie off the thread and cement the thread wraps.

If more weight is desired, use the **bead head** method (p. 51) to weight the fly and form the underbody. Then complete the fly.

Dubbed Bodies—Chenille Dubbing Loop

Fur Caddis Pupa

Hook: Pupa or nymph, 2X heavy, 2X long, sizes 8-14, weighted
Thread: Brown or black
Rib: Copper wire
Abdomen: Tan or olive dubbing
Thorax/Legs: Pine or red squirrel fur
Collar: Optional, cream or tan Antron yarn
Head: Optional, brass bead

Fur Mayfly Nymph

Hook: Nymph, 2X heavy, 2X long, sizes 6-14, weighted
Thread: Brown or black
Tail: Brown or tan hen hackle fibers
Rib: Copper wire
Abdomen: Brown, tan or olive dubbing
Wing case: Brown Thin Skin or Antron yarn
Thorax/Legs: Pine or red squirrel fur
Head: Optional, brass bead

Note: A fur chenille dubbing loop is made from fur—cut from the hide with the guard hairs and underfur intact—that is placed perpendicular to the thread inside the dubbing loop and then spun into a chenille. A dubbing loop collar can be made using this same technique; for a fur collar, use just the longer hair without the underfur, or use any other soft, long-fibered material in the loop. Fur chenilles are ideal for forming spiky thoraxes or collars; for bodies, it is easier to use a **wire-core dubbing brush** (p. 30). You can take the fur right from a hide, but precut fur strips are easier to use.

Fur Caddis Pupa

Step 1. Mount a hook in the vise. Use the **underbody direct wrap** method (p. 20) to weight the body. Advance the thread to the rear. Mount a length of copper wire at the rear tie-in position and trim the excess.

Step 2. Use one of the dubbing methods to dub the abdomen. Counter-wrap the copper wire over the abdomen, secure it and trim the excess. Using the **dubbing loop** method (p. 28), form a thread loop 2-3 inches in length and hang the dubbing hook on it.

Step 3. Position the thread 4-6 thread wraps behind the hook eye. Pinch a small length of fur half way down its length with your left fingers; cut the fur close to the hide to free it.

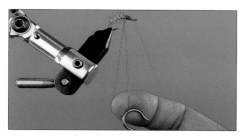

Step 4. Take the dubbing hook in your right hand and use your forefinger to open the loop as shown.

Step 5. Place the bunch of fur in the open loop as shown. Close the loop by carefully removing your right finger while taking up the slack with the dubbing hook.

Step 6. With the fur trapped in the loop, it is possible to carefully adjust its position. To allow unrestricted spinning of the fur, keep it about an inch below the hook shank. Position the fur so that the thread traps the lower half of the hairs.

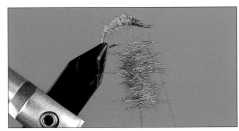

Step 7. Use the dubbing hook to spin the loop in a clockwise direction until a chenille is formed. Do not overspin the loop or you may break the thread.

Step 8. Wrap the fur chenille over the thorax, preening back the fibers as shown with each wrap. If more chenille is needed, secure the finished loop trim the excess and repeat Steps 2-7.

Step 9. Secure the chenille at the front tie-off position and trim the excess. Tie-off the thread and finish the head. Then trim the fur on top and sides as shown.

Optional: Bead Head Fur Caddis Pupa

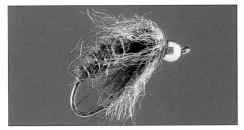

A bead may be used to add weight and flash to the fly. An Antron collar is used to imitate the pupal shuck.

Step 1. Use the **bead head** method (p. 51) to mount the bead. Follow Steps 1-9, but do not cut the thread. Form a 3-inch dubbing loop and hang the hook in it. Brush out a length of Antron yarn 1 1/2 times the length of the hook shank.

Step 2. Cut the brushed-out Antron from the yarn strand, place it in the loop, and spin it as shown above in Steps 4-7. Wrap the Antron chenille in front of the thorax, preening back the fibers with each wrap. Only 1 or 2 wraps are needed.

Fur Mayfly Nymph

Step 3. Secure the loop behind the bead. Use a short length of dubbed thread to cover the thread wraps behind the bead. Tie off the thread and finish the head.

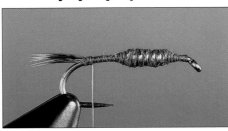

Step 1. Mount a hook in the vise. Use the **underbody direct wrap** (p. 20) method to weight the body. Advance the thread to the rear. **Align and strip** (p. 22) 4-10 barbs, from a hen feather; mount them at the rear tie-in position and trim the excess.

Step 2. Mount a length of copper wire at the rear tie-in position and trim the excess. Use one of the dubbing methods to form the abdomen, stopping at the middle of the hook shank. Counter-wrap the copper wire, secure it and trim the excess.

Bead Head Fur Mayfly Nymph

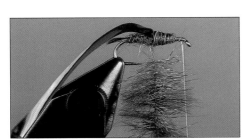

Step 3. Cut a strip of Thin Skin that is as wide as the hook gap. Mount it shiny side up, at the tie-in position and trim the excess. Form a dubbing loop and follow Steps 2-8 to form the chenille.

Step 4. Wrap the chenille forward, preening back the fibers; secure the dubbing loop and trim the excess. Preen the fibers down; pull the Thin Skin strip forward and secure it, Trim the excess, tie-off the thread and finish the head.

Use the **bead head** method (p. 51) to mount the bead, and complete the fly as shown above. Use brown Antron yarn for the wing case.

Dubbed Bodies—Noodle Dubbing Loop

Muskrat

Originator: Polly Rosborough
Hook: Nymph, 2X heavy, 3X long, sizes 6-16, weighted
Thread: Black
Body: Muskrat fur
Legs: Speckled guinea hackle fibers
Head: Black ostrich herl

Noodle Body Stonefly Nymph

Hook: Nymph, 2X heavy, 3X long, sizes 4-12, weighted
Thread: Brown or black
Tail: Brown or black goose biots
Abdomen: Brown or black dubbing
Wing case: Hen feathers, burned or cut to shape, coated with Flexament
Thorax: Brown or black dubbing
Legs: Brown or black round rubber
Head: Brown or black dubbing
Antennae: Brown or black goose biots

Note: This method works best with medium-fibered to long-fibered dubbing. A noodle formed with short-fibered dubbing will break apart. The shape of the noodle defines the shape of the body, while the tightness of the twist in the loop will govern how prominent the segments are. This method is a quick and easy way to tie large, segmented bodies. With slippery material, moisten your fingers for additional grip. Use a strong thread (6/0-3/0) with this method to avoid breaking the thread when twisting the loop.

Muskrat

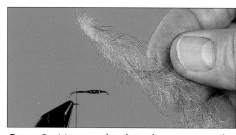

Step 1. Mount a hook in the vise. Use the **underbody direct wrap** method (p. 20) to weight the body. Advance the thread to the rear. Tease out an elongated skein of dubbing, tapering one end as shown.

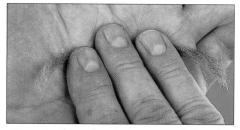

Step 2. Place the skein in your left palm. With your right fingers, compress the dubbing and roll it forward in your palm to tighten the skein. When the edge of your palm is reached, roll the skein back to the center of your palm.

Step 3. Move your fingers to compress another part of the skein. Repeat Steps 2 and 3 until the entire skein is rolled into a tight noodle. Make the noodle as even as possible; if a thin spot develops add dubbing to the area and roll it in.

Step 4. Mount the tapered end of the noodle at the rear tie-in position.

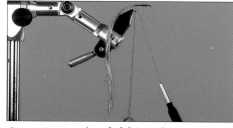

Step 5. Use the **dubbing loop** method (p. 28) to form a loop a little longer than the noodle. Hang the dubbing hook in the bottom of the loop. Advance the thread to the forward tie-off position.

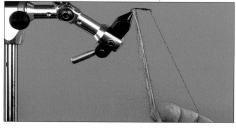

Step 6. Grip the dubbing hook in your right hand and open the loop with your right forefinger as shown. Gently place the noodle in the loop.

Step 7. Slide your finger out of the loop, trapping the noodle. Twist the noodle clockwise into a tight cord.

Step 8. Use close, tight wraps to wind the dubbing cord forward to the front tie-off position. Secure the cord and trim the excess.

Step 9. Align and cut (p. 22) 8-12 barbs from a guinea feather, and use the **bundled-fiber throat legs** method (p. 38) to mount them under the hook shank at the tie-in position.

Noodle Body Stonefly Nymph

Step 10. Trim the excess barbs. Mount an ostrich herl one inch back from its tip, and trim the excess. Advance the thread, stopping 4-5 thread wraps behind the hook eye.

Step 11. Wrap the herl forward to the tie-off position and secure it with 3 thread wraps. Trim the excess herl, tie off the thread, and finish the head.

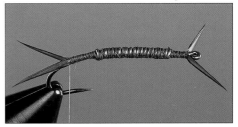

Step 1. Mount a hook in the vise. Use the **underbody direct wrap** method (p. 20) to weight the body. Use the **spit tail** method (p. 25) to mount biots behind the hook eye and at the rear of the hook. Place the thread at the rear tie-in position.

Step 2. Use Steps 1-8 shown above to form the abdomen, stopping at the middle of the hook shank. Take 5 tight thread wraps over the cord. Advance the thread to the forward tie-off position. Twist the cord counterclockwise to loosen it.

Step 3. Wrap the cord forward to the tie-off position, forming a smooth thorax. Secure the cord and trim the excess.

Step 4. Wind the thread back to the rear of the thorax. Use the **burned wing case** method (p. 40) to form 2 wing cases and coat them with Flexament. Mount one wing case on top of the thorax at the tie-in position and trim the excess.

Step 5. Use the **side-lashed single-fiber leg** method (p. 37) to mount the rubber legs over the thread wraps used to mount the wing case. Place a small amount of dubbing on the thread and dub over the exposed wraps, continuing to the position shown.

Step 6. Mount the second wing case with 4 tight thread wraps at the tie-in position. Fold the bottom of the feather back and wind the thread forward, stopping 4-5 thread wraps behind the hook eye. Pull the feather forward and secure it with 3 thread wraps.

Step 7. Trim the excess feather. Place a small amount of dubbing on the thread and dub over the thread wraps to form the head. Tie-off the thread and cement the thread wraps.

Chapter 6

Bead, Pulled, Stack, Spun and Woven Bodies

The body types shown in this chapter can be used as examples for tying similar patterns or designing ones that will fit your needs. There are many variations of these bodies, but once you learn the basic method you should be able to duplicate them.

Bead Bodies

Glass Bead Larva

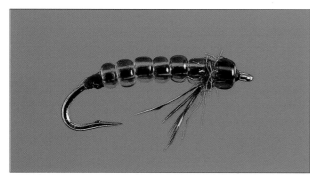

Hook: Nymph, 2X heavy, 2X-3X long, sizes 8-14
Thread: Brown and olive
Abdomen: Olive or tan glass beads
Legs: Brown hen hackle fibers
Head: Brown glass bead, Option: brass bead

Glass Bead Caddis Pupa

Hook: Nymph or scud, 2X heavy, 2X long, sizes 10-14
Thread: Tan or green
Rib: Cream or tan long-fibered Antron dubbing
Abdomen: Tan or green glass beads
Thorax: Brown Hare-Tron dubbing
Wings: Brown or black Antron yarn
Legs: CDC fibers
Head: Brass bead

Note: Glass beads come in a wide variety of sizes, colors, and transparencies, making it easy to create a pattern to match most nymphs, larvae, or pupae. To mount the bead, the hole must slide over the hook barb and around the bend of the hook. You can eliminate the barb by using a barbless hook or pinching down the barb. It is not advisable to bend the hook when installing the bead; you may weaken or break the hook. The thread underbody is used to center the bead and secure it. Handling beads can be difficult; in **bead head** methods (p. 51) there are instructions on modifying a pair of tweezers to grip beads.

Glass Bead Larva

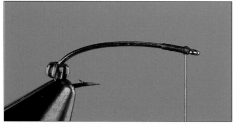

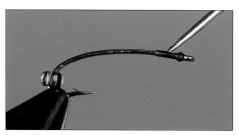

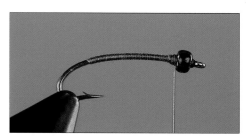

Step 1. Slide the brown bead on the hook. Mount the hook in the vise. Tie in the brown thread behind the hook eye and wind it back 2 bead lengths, then wind the thread back to the eye and build up a thread bump as shown.

Step 2. Slide the bead onto the thread wraps; if it is too loose, add another layer of thread. Continue building layers of thread until the bead fits snugly but still slides easily. Tie off the thread behind the hook eye, cut the thread, and cement the wraps.

Step 3. Push the bead against the thread bump. Tie in the green thread behind the bead. Wrap the thread over the hook shank forming an underbody with the same thickness of layered thread used in Step 2. Build a thread bump behind the bead.

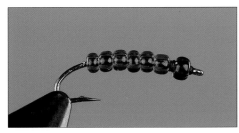

Step 4. Tie off the thread and cement the wraps. Take the hook from the vise and slide the body beads onto the hook. Mount the hook in the vise, and push the beads forward against the thread bump.

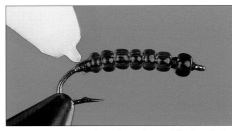

Step 5. Tie in the olive thread behind the last bead and build up a tapered thread bump to secure the bead. Tie off and cut the thread. Coat the thread wraps with CA glue to keep the thread bump in place.

Step 6. Tie in the thread behind the brown bead. **Align and strip** (p. 21) 6-8 barbs from a hen feather. Use the **bundled-fiber throat legs** method (p. 38) to mount the hen feather barbs on the bottom of the hook shank.

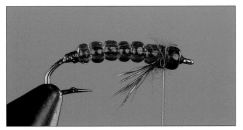

Step 7. Trim the excess feather barbs. Place a small amount of dubbing on the thread and dub over the thread wraps. Tie off the thread behind the bead. Cut the thread and cement the thread wraps.

Optional: Brass & Glass Bead Larva

Using a brass bead for the head is the only way to weight this fly. Use the **bead head** method (p. 51) to mount a counter-drilled bead, but use only enough lead wire to center the bead. Then complete the fly as shown above in Steps 4-7.

Glass Bead Caddis Pupa

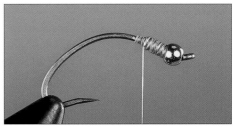

Step 1. Slide a counterdrilled brass bead onto the hook and mount the hook in the vise. Use the **bead head** method (p. 51) to secure the brass bead behind the hook eye.

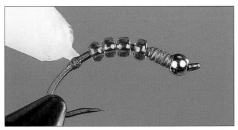

Step 2. Form the thread underbody for the glass beads and mount the 3-4 beads as shown above in Steps 2-4. Tie in the thread and build up a tapered thread bump at the rear of the body. Tie off the thread and use CA glue to coat the thread wraps.

Step 3. Push the rear bead against the thread bump. Tie in the thread in front of the bead and form a small bump against the bead. Place a small amount of Antron dubbing on the thread and dub a small ball that is a little thicker than the bead.

Step 4. Push the next bead against the dubbed ball. Wrap the thread in front of the bead and form small thread bump in front of the bead.

Step 5. Repeat Steps 3-4 to complete the abdomen. Dub another Antron dubbing ball in front of the last bead. Use brown dubbing to dub the thorax area.

Step 6. Use a **dubbing teaser** (p. 30) to brush out the dubbing; trim any overly long fibers. Use the **Antron wing bud** method (p. 44) to mount and form the wings.

Step 7. Use the **bundled-fiber throat legs** method (p. 38) to mount the CDC fibers. Trim the excess fibers. Use a small amount of brown dubbing to dub over the thread wraps. Tie off the thread behind the bead and cement the thread wraps.

Bead, Pulled, Stack, Spun and Woven Bodies—Pulled

Deep Sparkle Pupa

Originator: Gary LaFontaine
Hook: Nymph, 2X heavy, 2X long, sizes 10-16, weighted
Thread: Black
Overbody: Light yellow Antron yarn, or color to match natural
Underbody: Green Antron dubbing, or color to match natural
Legs: Brown hen hackle fibers
Head: Brown marabou herls or brown dubbing
Optional head: Brass bead

Krystal Flash Deep Pupa

Hook: Nymph, 2X heavy, 2X long, sizes 10-16
Thread: Black
Overbody: Green Krystal Flash, or color to match natural
Overbody: Gray Antron yarn, or color to match natural
Legs: Black or brown hen hackle fibers
Antennae: Natural CDC fibers
Head: Black or brown dubbing
Optional head: Brown glass bead

Note: While doing underwater studies of emerging caddisflies, Gary LaFontaine noticed a sparkle that was caused by sunlight reflected from the pupal shuck of the caddis. To imitate the sparkle from the shuck, Gary developed the pulled Antron overbody for his caddis pupa patterns. I think this is one of the best caddis pupa imitations available to anglers. The Krystal Flash Deep Pupa is a brighter, unweighted version of the original. Antron yarn is available as a single strand wrapped on a spool or carded as a multi-ply yarn that must be separated into single strands.

Deep Sparkle Pupa

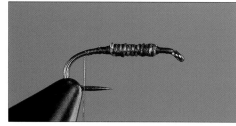

Step 1. Mount a hook in the vise. Use the **underbody direct wrap** method (p. 20) to weight the body. Advance the thread to the rear.

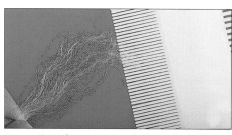

Step 2. Take a 2- 3-inch strand of Antron yarn, and use a fine-tooth comb (shown is a plastic flea comb, available at pet stores) to separate the fibers as shown.

Step 3. Mount the strand on the far side of the hook shank.

Step 4. Comb out another 2- 3-inch strand of yarn; mount it on the near side of the hook shank, and bind down all the excess fibers. Wrap the thread back to the rearmost thread wraps.

Step 5. Dub the underbody, stopping about 12 thread wraps behind the hook eye. Use the **dubbing teaser** (p. 29) to lightly brush out the body as shown.

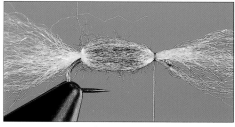

Step 6. Draw the near side yarn strand forward, keeping the strand fibers spread. At the front tie-in position, secure the yarn to the side of the hook shank with 2 thread wraps.

Step 7. Repeat Step 6 with the far side strand. Do not trim the excess. Use a dubbing needle to pull out the fibers to form the bubble. If you make a mistake you can pull the yarn tight and start over.

Step 8. Take 3-4 tight thread wraps to secure the yarn strands and trim the excess. At the front of the bubble, cut a few fibers from the top and sides and preen them back as shown.

Step 9. Align and cut (p. 22) 4-6 barbs from a hen feather and use the **bundled-fiber leg** method (p. 37) to mount the barbs on the near side of the hook shank at the tie-in position.

Step 10. Repeat Step 9 to mount the legs on the far side of the hook shank and trim the excess. Mount 4-8 marabou herls by their tips and trim the excess.

Step 11. Wrap the marabou forward and secure it with 3 thread wraps. Trim the excess, tie off the thread, and finish the head.

B/H Deep Sparkle Pupa

Add a brass bead to give the fly a little more weight and sparkle. Use the **bead head** method (p. 51) to secure the bead and form the underbody. Complete the fly as shown above, but use dubbing for the head. Tie off the thread behind the bead.

Krystal Flash Deep Pupa

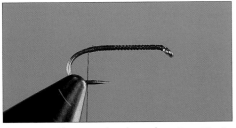

Step 1. Mount a hook in the vise. Tie in the thread at the front of the hook shank and wind the thread to the rear.

Step 2. Secure the brushed-out yarn strands as shown above in Steps 2-4. Mount 3-6 strands of Krystal Flash at the rear tie-in position and trim the excess. Wind the thread to the forward tie-off position.

Step 3. Grip the ends of the Krystal Flash with your fingers and twist them counter-clockwise into a tight cord. Wrap the Krystal Flash forward to form the underbody. Secure the Krystal Flash at the front tie-off position.

Step 4. Trim the excess Krystal Flash. Form the bubble and secure the legs as shown above in steps 6-9. Mount 4-6 CDC fibers on top of the hook shank as shown.

Step 5. Trim the excess CDC fibers and dub over the thread wraps to form the head. Tie off the thread and finish the head.

Glass Bead Head K.F. Deep Pupa

Use the **glass bead head** method (p. 51) to mount the bead. Then complete the fly as shown above.

Bead, Pulled, Stacked, Spun and Woven Bodies—Stacked Wool

Glo Bug

Hook: Nymph, 2X heavy, 1X short, sizes 6-14
Thread: 3/0 or stronger, color to match yarn
Body: Glo Bug Yarn, 3-6 pieces

Wool Dragonfly Nymph

Hook: Nymph, 2X heavy, 3X-4X long
Thread: Black 3/0 or stronger
Abdomen: Olive and light olive Sculpin Wool
Wing case: Green Thin Skin
Thorax/Head: Olive Sculpin Wool
Legs: Green rubber legs
Eyes: Lead eyes

Note: Stacked materials are easily trimmed to shape to form dense, durable bodies. The advantages of this method are the variety of materials that can be used, ranging from deer hair, to marabou, to yarns, and the ease of producing color variations. The above patterns are made from prepackaged materials, but you can use almost any long-fibered material with this method. Gauge the amount of fibers needed by twisting them into a tight cord; it should be about 2 to 4 times the thickness of the hook wire. It helps to comb out the material before using it. A strong thread is also necessary for this method.

Glo Bug

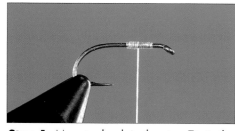

Step 1. Mount a hook in the vise. Tie in the thread a short distance back from the hook eye. Take 10-15 close tight thread wraps to the rear, then wrap the thread forward to the middle of the thread base.

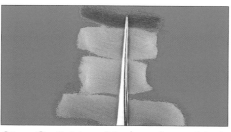

Step 2. Cut two 1-inch and one 2-inch lengths of Glo Bug Yarn, and a 1-inch length of red yarn that is about 1/2 the thickness of the Glo Bug Yarn.

Step 3. Center the 2-inch length of the Glo Bug Yarn over the mounting position and take 2 thread wraps over the yarn. Pull the thread straight down, as it tightens the yarn will spin to the underside of the hook shank.

Step 4. Stack the remaining yarn together with the red length on top and center the bundle over the tie-in position. With light tension take one thread wrap over the bundles. The thread wrap should be directly atop the other two.

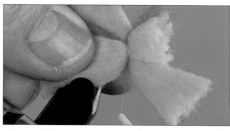

Step 5. Place your left forefinger on the far side of the hook shank to hold the bundle in position and pull the straight down on the thread to tighten the wrap. Take two more tight thread wraps, placing them directly on top of the previous wraps.

Step 6. While keeping tension on the thread, work it through the yarn. When the thread is clear, preen back the yarn and take 5 tight thread wraps against the base of the yarn. Tie off the thread and cement the wraps.

Wool Dragonfly Nymph

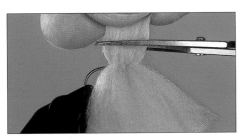

Step 7. With your left fingers preen up the top lengths of yarn. While holding the yarn vertical to the hook shank, measure about 2/3 the distance of the hook gap and cut the yarn parallel to the hook shank

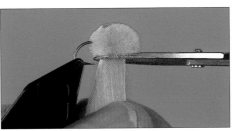

Step 8. Repeat Step 7 with the lower length of yarn.

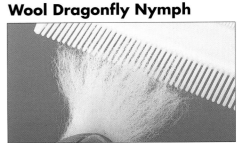

Step 1. Cut a one-inch length of light olive Sculpin Wool. To prepare it for mounting, hold it by one end and gently comb through it to align the fibers. Then change ends and comb out the other end.

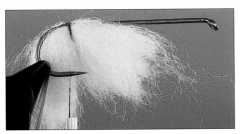

Step 2. Mount a hook in the vise. Tie in the thread at the rear of the hook and build a thread base as shown above in Step 1. Center the prepared wool clump over the tie-in position and mount it as shown above in Step 2.

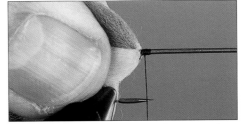

Step 3. Prepare a bundle of olive Sculpin Wool and center it over the tie-in position and mount it as shown above in Steps 4-5. Work the thread though the wool; preen back the wool and take 5 thread wraps forward, then wrap the thread back 3 wraps.

Step 4. Repeat Steps 1-3 until 3/4 of the hook shank is covered. Tie-off the thread and cement the thread wraps.

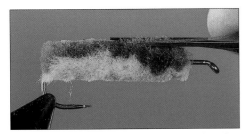

Step 5. Trim the top, bottom and sides flat. The bottom length should be less than half the hook gap to ensure hooking effectiveness.

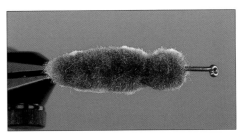

Step 6. Round off the corners and shape the body.

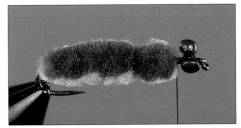

Step 7. Tie in the thread behind the hook eye. Use the **eye mounting** method (p. 50) to mount the eyes. Wind the thread to the rear as shown.

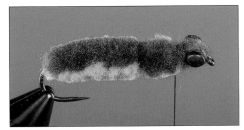

Step 8. Use one of the dubbing methods to dub the thorax and around the eyes. Leave the thread at the rear of the thorax.

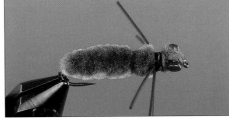

Step 9. Use the **side-lashed single-fiber** method (p. 37) to mount the rubber legs. After mounting the legs, fold the front legs down and to the rear; secure them with 3-4 thread wraps.

Step 10. Cut a Thin Skin strip as wide as the thorax and shape the end as shown. Mount the strip and trim the excess. Dub over the thread wraps. Advance the thread to the hook eye. Tie off the thread and finish the head.

Bead, Pulled, Stacked, Spun and Woven Bodies—Spun Deer Hair

Strawman

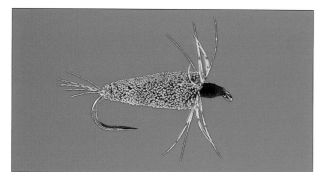

Originator: Paul Young
Hook: Nymph, 2X heavy, 2X-3X long, sizes 8-14, weight optional
Thread: Brown 6/0 or stronger
Tail: Mallard flank fibers
Body: Deer hair
Hackle: Gray partridge
Head: Brown thread

Floating Dragonfly Nymph

Originator: Randall Kaufmann
Hook: Nymph, 3X-4X long, sizes 4-10
Thread: Olive or brown, 6/0 or stronger
Tail: Olive or brown marabou
Body: Olive or brown deer hair
Legs: Olive or brown marabou
Wing case: Turkey feather section, cut to shape and coated with Flexament
Eyes: Black plastic
Head: Olive or brown dubbing

Note: Though not often used for nymph patterns, spun hollow hair from antelope, caribou, and deer can be used to form bulky light bodies. When fishing, weight is added up the leader from the fly to sink it. The buoyancy of these bodies will cause the fly to float above the weight. This allows a fly to be fished above submerged rocks or weeds without snagging.

Strawman

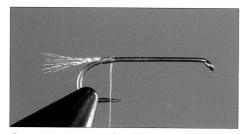

Step 1. Mount a hook in the vise. Tie in the thread at the rear of the hook. **Align and cut** (p. 22) 6-10 feather fibers for the tail. Extend the fibers half the hook shank length behind the tie-in position, mount them, and trim the excess.

Step 2. Advance the thread to the rear. Clean and stack a clump of deer hair that, when compressed between your fingers, is about half the width of the hook gap. Cut off the tips so the hair is about 3/4 inch in length.

Step 3. Grip the ends of the hair with your left fingers and center the bundle over the hanging thread.

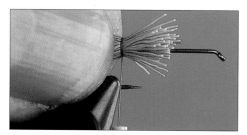

Step 4. Take two thread wraps around the middle of the bundle, placing the wraps on top of one another. The thread tension should be just enough to hold the hair in place.

Step 5. Slowly apply tension to the thread as you lift the bobbin to start another wrap. As the hair starts to flare, remove your left fingers and allow the hair to spin around the hook shank. Continue to tighten the thread, following the spinning hair.

Step 6. Increase the tension on the thread and continue the slow wraps around the center of the bundle until it no longer spins. At this point, the flared hair is now secured and should be evenly spread around the hook shank.

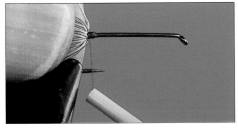

Step 7. Preen back the hair and draw the thread to the front of the bundle. Take 3-4 thread wraps against the base of the bundle.

Step 8. Repeat the above Steps 2-7 and mount another bundle of hair. To form a dense body, compress the hair by pushing back at the base of the front hairs with your right fingers while your left fingers hold the base of the rear bundle.

Step 9. Repeat the above Steps 2-8 until you have covered 3/4 of the hook shank. Tie off the thread and cement the wraps.

Step 10. Trim the body to a cone shape. Take care not to cut the tail fibers. Tie in the thread behind the hook eye and wrap it back to the body. Prepare a feather as shown.

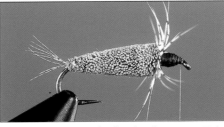

Step 11. Mount the feather by its tip. Take one wrap, secure it, and trim the excess. Build up a thread head as shown. Tie off the thread and finish the head.

Floating Dragonfly Nymph

Step 1. Mount a hook in the vise. Tie in the thread at the rear of the hook shank. **Align and cut** (p. 22) a bundle of marabou fibers. Extend the fibers a short distance behind the bend of the hook and mount them at the tie-in position. Trim the excess fibers.

Step 2. Follow the above Steps 2-9 to spin the deer-hair body over the rear 3/4 of the hook shank. On larger hook sizes, use hair that is an inch or more in length.

Step 3. Trim the hair on the top and bottom flat. Then taper the top slightly to the rear

Step 4. Trim the sides to a taper, making the front as wide as the plastic eyes.

Step 5. Tie in the thread in front of the body. Use the **bundled-fiber legs** method (p. 37) to mount the marabou fibers. Trim the excess fibers. Use the **eye mounting** method (p. 50) to mount the eyes.

Step 6. Dub around the eyes and thorax. Finish with the thread in front of the body. Use the **cut wing case** method (p. 39) to make a wing case that is as wide as the body.

Step 7. Mount the wing case on top of the body at the tie-in position as shown, and trim the excess. Place a small amount of dubbing on the thread and dub over the thread wraps and forward to the hook eye. Tie off the thread and finish the head.

Bead, Pulled, Stacked, Spun, and Woven Bodies—Overhand Weave

Woven Caddis Larva

Hook: Shrimp or nymph, 2X heavy, 2X long, sizes 8-14, weighted
Thread: Brown
Abdomen: Olive and tan Ultra Chenille
Thorax: Olive dubbing
Legs: Olive CDC fibers
Head: Brown dubbing

Woven Stonefly Nymph

Hook: Nymph, 2X heavy, 3X-4X long, sizes 6-12, weighted
Thread: Brown
Tail: Brown goose biots
Abdomen: Gold and brown Vinyl Rib
Wing case: Turkey feather section
Thorax: Brown dubbing
Legs: Brown hen or rooster saddle feather
Head: Brown dubbing

Note: The overhand weave is easy to learn. The durable bodies formed with this weave are oval in shape, and when two different colored strands are used, it produces bicolor body with a distinct edge. Many different materials can be used with this weave, and it is ideal for forming distinctive nymph bodies.

Woven Caddis Larva

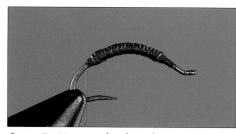

Step 1. Mount a hook in the vise. Use the **underbody direct wrap** method (p. 20) to weight the body. Advance the thread to the rear.

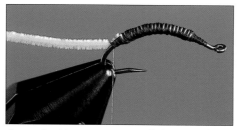

Step 2. Mount a 3- 6-inch length of tan chenille on the far side of the hook shank. Bind the tag end to the side of the hook shank up to the lead wraps, and trim the excess. Return the thread to the rear.

Step 3. Mount a 3- 6-inch length of olive chenille on the near side of the hook as shown in Step 2. Trim the excess chenille. Wrap the thread forward to the hook eye. Tie off and cut the thread.

Step 4. Position the vise so the hook eye is facing you. Form an overhand knot on the bottom of the hook shank as shown.

Step 5. Form a "loop" with the olive chenille. The olive strand will be used to form the top of the body, and all other knot "loops" must be formed with this strand.

Step 6. Guide the "loop" over the hook eye.

Step 7. Tighten the knot over the rear thread wraps by pulling evenly outward on the strands. The strands are now reversed from their original positions shown in Step 3.

Step 8. Tie the next overhand knot. Form a "loop" with the olive strand.

Step 9. Insert the "loop" over the hook eye. Slide the loop against the first knot, and pull outward on the strands with even pressure to tighten the knot. The strands are now back in their original positions.

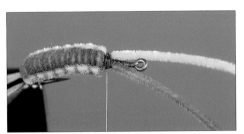

Step 10. Repeat Steps 4-9 until the abdomen is covered. Tie in the thread behind the hook eye. Wind the back to the front of the body and secure the strands of chenille to the sides of the hook shank.

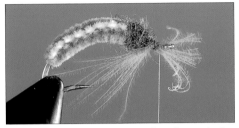

Step 11. Trim the excess chenille. Dub the thorax. Use the **bundled-fiber throat legs** method (p. 38) to mount the CDC fibers on the bottom of the hook shank.

Step 12. Trim the excess CDC fibers. Dub the head, tie off the thread, and finish the head.

Woven Stonefly Nymph

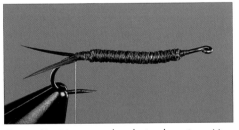

Step 1. Mount a hook in the vise. Use the **underbody direct wrap** method (p. 20) to weight the fly. Advance the thread to the rear. Use the **split tail** method (p. 25) to mount the biots, trim the excess.

Step 2. Mount the Vinyl Rib as shown above in Steps 2-3 with the gold strand on the far side and the brown strand on the near side. Complete the abdomen as shown above in Steps 4-11. Vinyl Rib stretches, so use care in tightening the knots.

Step 3. Prepare a feather section as wide as the hook gap and coat it with Flexament. Mount the feather section at the tie-in position, wrap the thread back to secure it over the first body segment. Mount a hen saddle feather by its tip at the tie-in position.

Step 4. Dub the thorax. Wind the feather forward 3-4 wraps; secure it at the front tie-off position and trim the excess.

Step 5. Preen the feather barbs down; pull the feather section forward and secure it. Then bind the tag end to the hook shank, stopping the thread wraps behind the hook eye.

Step 6. Dub the head, and leave the thread in front of the thorax. Fold the feather section toward the rear and secure it at the tie-off position. Trim the feather section a short distance back from the thread wraps. Tie off the thread and cement the wraps.

FLY INDEX

FLY PATTERN GROUPS

Helpful Books for Your Fishing and Fly Tying Library

FEDERATION OF FLY FISHERS FLY PATTERN ENCYCLOPEDIA
Over 1600 of the Best Fly Patterns
Edited by Al & Gretchen Beatty

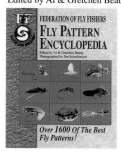

Simply stated, this book is a Federation of Fly Fishers' conclave taken to the next level, a level that allows the reader to enjoy the learning and sharing in the comfort of their own home. The flies, ideas, and techniques shared herein are from the "best of the best" demonstration fly tiers North America has to offer. The tiers are the famous as well as the unknown with one simple characteristic in common; they freely share their knowledge. Many of the unpublished patterns in this book contain materials, tips, tricks, or gems of information never before seen.

As you leaf through these pages, you will get from them just what you would if you spent time in the fly tying area at any FFF function. At such a show, if you dedicate time to observing the individual tiers, you can learn the information, tips, or tricks they are demonstrating. All of this knowledge can be found in *Federation of Fly Fishers Fly Pattern Encyclopedia* so get comfortable and get ready to improve upon your fly tying technique with the help of some of North America's best fly tiers. Full color, 8 1/2 x 11 inches, 232 pages.

SB: $39.95   ISBN: 1-57188-208-1
SPIRAL HB: $49.95   ISBN: 1-57188-209-X

FISHING JOURNAL: ANGLING LEGACY

Write, for future generations, about yourself and the stream. Use this attractive hard-bound book to record your days on the water for future use by yourself, relatives, or friends. It will become a treasured family document as it is handed down through your family. Each printed page contains spaces for entries such as: location, companion, weather, water conditions, fishing equipment, hatches, flies or lures, special fish sizes, species, etc. In addition there is much lined space for trip observations—what future readers will especially enjoy. Wouldn't you have liked to have read your grandfather's fishing journal? Start yours now! With ribbon and round back case binding, 6 x 9 inches, 240 pages.

SB: $19.95   ISBN: 1-57188-211-1

CENTURY END: A FLY TYING JOURNEY
Paul Ptalis

Atlantic salmon flies are exquisite works of art with a history that is as interesting as it is full of tradition. This gorgeous book takes us back in time to England, Ireland, and Scotland when the original Spey and classic Atlantic salmon flies were originated and flourished as "fishing" flies. Each of the 34 glorious flies are pictured at almost half-page in size, and each includes the recipe and originator. Also included is hook information—both antique and contemporary—artistic tying suggestions, and more. This full-color book is useful to the tier and a beautiful addition to the library of any fly fisherman.

SB: $19.95   ISBN: 1-57188-218-9

THE FLY TIER'S BENCHSIDE REFERENCE TO TECHNIQUES AND DRESSING STYLES
Ted Leeson and Jim Schollmeyer

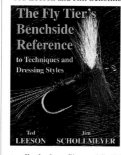

Printed in full color on top-quality paper, this book features over 3,000 color photographs and over 400,000 words describing and showing, step-by-step, hundreds of fly-tying techniques! Leeson and Schollmeyer have collaborated to produce this masterful volume which will be the standard fly-tying reference book for the entire trout-fishing world. Through enormous effort on their part they bring to all who love flies and fly fishing a wonderful compendium of fly-tying knowledge. Every fly tier should have this book in their library! All color, 8 1/2 by 11 inches, 464 pages, over 3,000 color photographs, index, hardbound with dust jacket.

HB: $100.00.   ISBN: 1-57188-126-3

WHICH FLY DO I USE?
Darren Banasch

With thousands upon thousands of fly patterns in existence, the question of which to use is a good one. It is impossible for the avid fly-fisher to know all the patterns and which to use in various waters, let alone the casual or beginning fly-fisher. Despite the wide variety of available fly patterns, it *is* possible to choose a selection of appropriate flies that are proven producers on all three water types in which trout are found—streams, rivers, and lakes. *Which Fly Do I Use?* also includes: fly tackle, effective presentations, trout foods (including photos and illustrations), essential knots, and more. All for just $8.95!

Which Fly Do I Use? is a guide—for fly-fishers of all levels—to some of the best patterns that tempt trout. So whether you buy flies, or tie your own, this book will answer the question of which fly to use. Full color; 5 1/2 x 8 1/2 inches, 48 pages; individual fly plates; illustrations.

SB: $8.95   ISBN: 1-57188-202-2

HATCH GUIDE FOR NEW ENGLAND STREAMS
Thomas Ames, Jr.

New England's streams, and the insects and fish that inhabit them, have their own unique qualities. Their flowing waters support an amazing diversity of insect species from all of the major orders—in fact, at last count, Maine, alone, has 162 species of mayflies, the most of any state. Few, if any, books deal with the insects and life stages specific to New England, until now.

Hatch Guide to New England Streams, by professional photographer and "amateur entomology enthusiast" Thomas Ames, explores the insects of New England. Ames covers: reading water; presentations for New England streams; tackle; night fishing; and more. The bulk of this book, however, deals with the insects and the best flies to imitate them. Similar in style to Jim Schollmeyer's successful "Hatch Guide" series, Ames discusses the natural and its behaviors on the left-hand page and the three best flies to imitate it on the right, including proper size and effective techniques. Tom's color photography of the naturals and their imitations is superb, making this book as beautiful as it is useful. A must for all New England fly-fishers! Full color, 4 1/8 x 6 1/8 inches, 272 pages; insect and fly plates.

SB: $19.95   ISBN: 1-57188-210-3
HB: $29.95   ISBN: 1-57188-220-0

TROUT FLIES OF THE WEST: CONTEMPORARY PATTERNS FROM THE ROCKY MOUNTAINS, WEST
Jim Schollmeyer and Ted Leeson

This beautifully illustrated, all-color book features over 300 of the West's best specialty trout flies and their recipes and an explanation of each fly's use. The flies and information were researched from scores of the West's finest fly shops. Over 600 color photographs. The very latest word on the most effective Western patterns! 8 1/2 x 11, 128 pages.

SB: $34.95   ISBN: 1-57188-145-X

TROUT FLIES OF THE EAST
Jim Schollmeyer and Ted Leeson

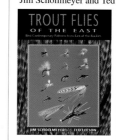

In fly fishing, there is no substitute for local knowledge. Walk into any fly shop and you will find "shop patterns"— flies local to the area. Far more often than not, these are the top choices for fishing rivers and lakes in a given area. Second in a series devoted to celebrating these flies, this book focuses on trout flies, although some are well-suited to steelhead, salmon, and warmwater species as well.

Patterns shared include: attractors and multi-purpose; mayflies; caddisflies; stoneflies; midges; damsel and dragonfly, hellgrammite, crustaceans; baitfish; leeches; terrestrials; and more. Once again, Jim and Ted provide top-quality writing and photography. Your fly-fishing library is not complete without this first-rate book. 8 1/2 x 11 inches; 128 pages. All color.

SB: $34.95   ISBN: 1-57188-196-4
SPIRAL HB: $44.95   ISBN: 1-57188-197-2

INSHORE FLIES: BEST CONTEMPORARY PATTERNS FROM THE ATLANTIC AND GULF COASTS
Jim Schollmeyer and Ted Leeson

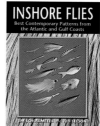

Inshore Flies is third in a series of three fly-pattern books created to introduce effective flies designed by knowledgeable local anglers and available in shops in a particular area—after all, no one knows better than these folks what patterns are most productive. Fly patterns are included for: New England states, Mid-Atlantic, Gulf states and Florida. Well-respected experts Jim and Ted collaborate once again to make this book a first-class project. 8 1/2 x 11 inches, 128 pages.

SB: $29.95   ISBN: 1-57188-193-X
SPIRAL HB: $39.95   ISBN: 1-57188-194-8

WHAT FISH SEE
Dr. Colin Kageyama, O.D.

An in-depth examination by Dr. Colin Kageyama of how and what fish see. This important book will help all anglers to design better flies and lures by its explanation of the physical processes of light in water and consequently how colors change and are perceived by fish in varying conditions of depth, turbidity, and light. Excellent illustrations by Vic Erickson and color plates that show startling color changes. This book will change the way you fish! 5 1/2 x 8 1/2 inches, 184 pages.

SB: $19.95   ISBN: 1-57188-140-9

Helpful Books for Your Fishing and Fly Tying Library

HATCH GUIDE FOR THE LOWER DESCHUTES RIVER
Jim Schollmeyer

The most valuable book you can own if you fly fish for trout. In excellent color photographs and precise text, Deschutes trout guide Jim Schollmeyer explains the intricate hatches and the nymphs and dries to use. You will want to carry this book with you everywhere along the Deschutes and other Western rivers for immediate, professional help. That's why we made it in a handy size with a hard cover. 4 x 5 inches, 112 pages.

HB: $19.95   **ISBN: 1-878175-71-8**

MODERN ATLANTIC SALMON FLIES
Paul Marriner

Featuring 300 individual, detailed, color photographs of the most popular and productive modern Atlantic salmon fly patterns, wets, drys, etc. Included are complete tying recipes for each fly as well as a history of its origin and fishing technique use. Extremely helpful for the non-tier as a source for selecting the best patterns for specific waters. 8 1/2 x 11 inches, 100 pages, all-color.

SB: $34.95   **ISBN: 1-57188-152-2**
SPIRAL HB: $44.95   **ISBN: 1-57188-153-0**
NUMBERED LIMITED EDITION SPIRAL HB: $75.00

STEELHEAD FLY TYING GUIDE
Kent Helvie

This is a gorgeous, all-color, step-by-step book that will make steelhead fly tying easy for you. Scores of crisp color photos show you how to tie all the most productive steelhead patterns including Speys, traditional wets, skaters, wakers, and dries. Beautiful color plates will excite you every time you look at them. Once you learn the different tying methods you will then be able to tie all the great patterns shown in the color plates. A magnificent book! 8 1/2 x 11 inches, 80 pages.

SB: $24.95   **ISBN: 1-878175-85-8**

FRONTIER FLIES: PATTERNS ON THE CUTTING EDGE
Troy Bachmann
Photographed by Jim Schollmeyer

Features the finest and most contemporary flies to tie and fish. All-color fly pattern book with over 600 cutting-edge flies (with dressings and fishing explanations) for virtually all sport-fishing situations. Also, narrative by Rick Hafele, Mark Bachmann, Dave Hughes, Bill McMillan, Tom Earnhardt, Brian O'Keefe. 8 1/2 by 11 inches, 128 pages.

SB: $29.95   **ISBN: 1-57188-129-8**
SPIRAL HB: $39.95   **ISBN: 1-57188-130-1**

HATCH GUIDE FOR LAKES: Naturals and Their Imitations for Stillwater Trout Fishing
Jim Schollmeyer

This "little lake Bible" organizes and explains lake types, how to read and fly fish them, and understand and imitate their aquatic insect life cycles—and nearby terrestrial insects. Next to each color insect photograph is a representative fly pattern. By carefully inspecting the lake for insects you can find the correct fly to use as shown in the book. *Hatch Guide for Lakes* is the golden key to unravelling one of fly fishing's last best-kept secrets. 4 x 5 inches, 162 pages.

HB: $21.95   **ISBN: 1-57188-038-0**

FLY PATTERNS FOR STILLWATERS
Philip Rowley

Phil has spent countless hours at lakes studying the food sources that make up the diet of trout; then set up home aquariums to more closely observe the movement, development, and emergence of the aquatic insects. In this book he explains the link between understanding the food base within lakes to designing effective fly patterns for these environs. Phil covers all major trout food sources for the whole year. He gives detailed information on each, plus how to tie a representative pattern and fish it effectively. Numerous proven stillwater patterns are given for each insect and include clear and concise tying instructions. This book will be a long-standing stillwater fly pattern reference for years to come. All-color, 8 1/2 x 11 inches, 104 pages.

SB: $29.95   **ISBN: 1-57188-195-6**

FLY TYING WITH POLY YARN
Lee Clark and Joe Warren

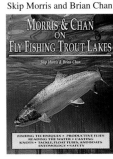

Over his many years of fly tying, Lee Clark has blended his knowledge of art with his skills as a fly tier to develop unique tying concepts using polypropylene (poly yarn). Poly yarn is buggy, buoyant, and blendable, the perfect material for tying effective fishing flies. *Fly Tying With Poly Yarn* shares all the information you need to tie effective flies, it includes: full-color step-by-step instructions for combing and mixing yarn; blending it for dubbing; yarn foundations; body wraps; yarn shrouds; wings; spinning and bundling yarn. Also step-by-step instructions for tying 12 fish-catching flies, including the Clark's Stonefly, and more than 85 patterns for imitating stoneflies, caddisflies, and mayflies, with individual fly plates by Jim Schollmeyer. Buggy, buoyant, blendable! *Fly Tying With Poly Yarn* will show you the best ways to utilize this perfect material for your tying needs. Full color, 8 1/2 x 11 inches, 56 pages.

SB: $19.95   **ISBN: 1-57188-201-4**

HATCH GUIDE FOR WESTERN STREAMS
Jim Schollmeyer

Successful fishing on Western streams requires preparation—you need to know what insects are emerging, when and where, and which patterns best match them. Now, thanks to Jim Schollmeyer, the guessing is over.

Hatch Guide for Western Streams is the third in Jim's successful "Hatch Guide" series. Jim covers all you need for a productive trip on Western streams: water types you'll encounter; successful fishing techniques; identifying the major hatches, providing basic background information about these insects. Information is presented in a simple, clear manner. A full-color photograph of the natural is shown on the left-hand page, complete with its characteristics, habits and habitat; the right-hand page shows three flies to match the natural, including effective fishing techniques. 4 x 5 inches; full-color; 196 pages; fantastic photographs of naturals and flies.

SB: $19.95   **ISBN: 1-57188-109-3**

MORRIS & CHAN ON FLY FISHING TROUT LAKES
Skip Morris and Brian Chan

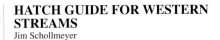

From two of the biggest names in the industry comes this all-encompassing guide to fly fishing trout lakes. Combining their vast knowledge on fly fishing, fly tying, entomology, and aquatic biology, Skip Morris and Brian Chan have created a book full of information for lake fly-fishers of all levels. They share: general techniques; reading a lake; cycles of a trout lake; insects and other trout foods; productive lake flies; casting; watercraft; equipment; knots; trout species; learning a new lake; courtesy and safety; and more.

With the teaming of Skip Morris and Brian Chan, you are getting the advice of top experts in the fields of fly fishing, fly tying, entomology, and fish biology. This is your guide for improving and perfecting your skills as a lake fly-fisher. All-color, 8 1/2 x 11 inches; 96 pages.

SB: $24.95   **ISBN: 1-57188-181-6**
HB: $39.95   **ISBN: 1-57188-182-4**

TYING GLASS BEAD FLIES
Joe Warren

Master glass-bead fly tier Joe Warren is doing his best to bring this innovative approach to more fly tiers. In *Tying Glass Bead Flies* he shares his vast knowledge, providing you with all you need to begin including glass beads in your flies. Joe shows you the best hooks and beads to use (including charts and color plates); the most effective tools and accessories; the different uses for beads and the techniques needed to incorporate them into your fly tying; tying instructions with hundreds of color photos; tons of tips; and hundreds of fly patterns for both fresh- and saltwater.

Fly tying by its very nature is an art form, adding glass beads brings it to a much higher level. Read *Tying Glass Bead Flies* to master this beautiful and functional way of tying effective flies. 8 1/2 x 11; full color; 64 pages.

SB: $19.95   **ISBN: 1-57188-107-7**

Helpful Books for Your Fishing and Fly Tying Library

NYMPH FISHING
Dave Hughes

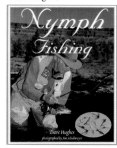

This masterful all-color, large format book by one of America's favorite angling writers will teach you what you need to know to fish nymphs effectively, with crisp text and dramatic color photos by Jim Schollmeyer. Color plates and dressings of author's favorite nymphs. All the techniques and methods learned here will guarantee that on the stream or lake your nymph imitation will be fishing right! 8 1/2 x 11 inches, 56 pages.
SB: $19.95   ISBN: 1-57188-002-X

ROD-BUILDING GUIDE: FLY, SPINNING, CASTING, TROLLING
Tom Kirkman

Tom Kirkman is editor of *Rod Maker* magazine. Think you need an engineering degree to build your own rod? Think again. Building your own rod is challenging, rewarding, and fun! Whether you're trying to while away the winter months, create the best-performing rod possible, or you are just trying to save a few bucks, *Rod-Building Guide* will show you how. Tom covers: blanks and components; rod-building tools; adhesive and bonding techniques; understanding rod spine; grip, handle, and seat assembly; guide placement, guide prep and wrapping; finishing; and more. This is a book a beginner can understand and from which an old pro can learn some new techniques. *Rod-Building Guide* will guarantee your rod-building experience is comfortable, successful, and fun.
SB: $14.95   ISBN: 1-57188-216-2

DRY FLY FISHING
Dave Hughes

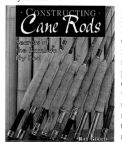

This beautifully written, all-color guide, will help make you a very competent dry-fly angler with chapters on: tackle, dry-fly selection, dry-fly casting techniques, fishing dry-flies on moving water and on lakes and ponds, hatches and matching patterns, and 60 of the best dries in color and with fly dressings. The information contained and attractive color presentation will really help you! 8 1/2 x 11 inches, 56 pages.
SB: $15.95   ISBN: 1-878175-68-8

CONSTRUCTING CANE RODS: SECRETS OF THE BAMBOO FLY ROD
Ray Gould

An all-color book by master rod builder, Ray Gould. Included is the history of cane, the creation of the machines and tools necessary to create your own rods, precise taper formulas, detailed schematic drawings with precise angles, step-by-step construction, finishing steps, formulas, repairs, historic cane manufacturers and model names, and address and phone sources for all materials. This is a masterful book filled with detailed information that will open up a new world for you. Full color, 8 1/2 x 11 inches, 88 pages.
SPIRAL HB: $39.95   ISBN: 1-57188-137-9

THE FISH BUM'S GUIDE TO CATCHING LARGER TROUT: AN ILLUSTRATED MANUAL ON STILLWATER TACTICS
Michael Croft

A brilliant explanation of how to fly fish still water, ponds, lakes, and reservoirs by a long-practiced expert. You will marvel at the inside information presented in a dramatic and hilarious drawing style. Valuable information about casting, reading water, lines, reels, rods, float equipment, flies, hatches, weather, structure. Hundreds of hand-drawn illustrations. 8 1/2 x 11 inches, 96 pages.
SB: $14.95   ISBN: 1-57188-142-5

A PERFECT FISH
Ken Abrames

Take your fly tying a step further; not only will you catch more stripers and other game fish, but tying flies will take on a more personal and satisfying dimension for you, and as we all know confidence is the name of the game. Abrames shares: the freedom and creativity in fly design; techniques for successful fly fishing; many productive patterns and how to tie them; much information on game fish behavior; deep insight into stripers and the flies that catch them; and more.

Abrames introduces you to a whole new level in fly tying—harnessing your creativity and intelligence to make for more effective flies. 8 1/2 x 11 inches; 110 pages.
SB: $29.95   ISBN: 1-57188-138-7
HB: $39.95   ISBN: 1-57188-179-4

Ask for these books at your local fly/tackle shop or call toll-free to order:
1-800-541-9498 (8-5 p.s.t.) • www.amatobooks.com
Frank Amato Publications, Inc. • P.O. Box 82112 • Portland, Oregon 97282

SPECIAL INVITATION

In addition to publishing the above books we also publish *Flyfishing & Tying Journal* which is devoted to the best fly-fishing techniques, flies and fishing opportunities in North America. We invite you to try it out! To receive a sample copy call 800-541-9498, e-mail us at paulette@amatobooks.com, or send your name and address to Frank Amato Publications, Inc. P.O. Box 82112, Portland, Oregon 97282.